NUMBERS
Journey to God's Rest-Land

NUMBERS

Journey to God's Rest-Land

By
IRVING L. JENSEN

MOODY PRESS
CHICAGO

ISBN: 0-8024-2004-4

Printed in the United States of America

To

My wife, Charlotte

CONTENTS

PREFACE

THE OBJECT of this book is to tell the events of Numbers as one story, showing how each of its chapters and segments fills an appointed place in the divinely inspired writing. Applications are made along the way, but the reader is encouraged to look for many more.

Most of the quotations from the Bible are from the American Standard Version. Quotations from the Berkeley Version are so indicated. For the Old Testament, the King James Version is very similar to the American Standard Version, due in part to the meticulous care of the Hebrew Masoretes in the transmission of the Old Testament text through the early centuries of the Christian era. For maximum profit the reader should refer to the Biblical text of Numbers as he proceeds through this book.

It is the sincere hope of the writer that the book will help to focus the light of God's revelation of Numbers on present-day Christian living.

IRVING L. JENSEN

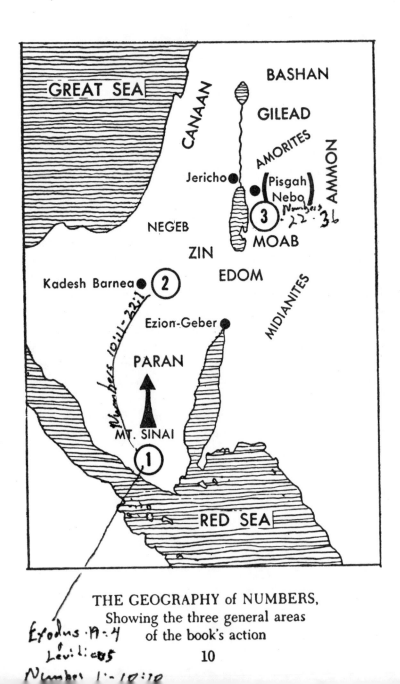

THE GEOGRAPHY of NUMBERS,
Showing the three general areas
of the book's action

10

Exodus 19:4
Leviticus
Numbers 1 - 10:10

INTRODUCTION

EVERY BOOK OF THE BIBLE is basically a record of *God speaking to man.* This holds true for the records of history, for the prayers of a man to God (Psalms), and for the letters of a man to various churches (e.g., Romans). Numbers is no exception. Its opening words are "And the Lord spake unto Moses," and its closing words are "These are the commandments . . . which the Lord commanded . . . unto the children of Israel" (36:13).

Down through the centuries the heart of man has remained the same. Nor has God changed—immutability is one of His eternal attributes. Therefore, that which God said to Moses and to the children of Israel millenniums ago, and which God inspired to be recorded in Numbers, is so meaningful to man today that he should know this part of the whole counsel of God.

Author and Title

Author. The traditional view has always been that Moses was the author of Numbers, even as he wrote the other four books of the Pentateuch. (The word *Pentateuch* literally means "fivefold vessel.") The list of witnesses through the centuries holding the view of Mosaic authorship of the Pentateuch is impressive. This list of witnesses includes: (1) the Jews and Samaritans of the fifth century B.C. (as confirmed by the Samaritan Pentateuch); (2) the Jewish tradition of subsequent centuries; (3) Jesus and the New Testament writers (cf. Matt. 8: 4; 19:8; Mark 1:44; 7:10; 10:4, 5; Luke 5:14; 16:31;

20:37; 24:27, 44; John 5:46, 47; 7:19; Acts 3:22; 13:39; 15:5-21; 26:22; 28:23; Rom. 10:5, 19; I Cor. 9:9; II Cor. 3:15; Rev. 15:3); (4) the early Christian church; (5) most Biblical scholars until the rise of the movement of modern higher criticism (begun in the middle of the eighteenth century).

The internal evidence of Mosaic authorship is also impressive. Considering the Pentateuch as a whole, there is a unity of contents and purpose that points to a single author, each book taking up where the previous book left off. Specific references to Mosaic authorship are found in three legislative sections (Exod. 17:14; 24:4-8; 34:27) and three historical sections (Num. 33:1, 2; Deut. 31:9; 31:22). Furthermore, Moses is the central character of the four books from Exodus to Deuteronomy, and there was no one better fitted to be the author, as to ability and experience (e.g., he was an eyewitness of the years in Egypt, in the desert, and in the wilderness). Other books of the Old Testament also refer to Mosaic authorship.

In the last two hundred years many theories have been proposed by liberal critics denying Mosaic authorship and attributing the writings to many authors, editors, or redactors during much later years.[1] Edward J. Young maintains, along with many other conservative scholars, that a satisfactory substitute for the traditional view of Mosaic authorship has not yet been produced.[2] Oswald

[1]For discussion of this and related subjects, see Oswald T. Allis, *The Five Books of Moses* (Philadelphia: Presbyterian and Reformed Publishing Co., 1949); Edward J. Young, *An Introduction to the Old Testament* (Grand Rapids: Wm. B. Eerdmans Publishing Co., 1949); and Merrill F. Unger, *Introductory Guide to the Old Testament* (Grand Rapids: Zondervan Publishing House, 1951), pp. 213-276.

[2]Young, *op. cit.,* p. 152.

T. Allis says that to deny such authorship is a serious error because (1) positive external evidence is rejected in the interest of a mere theory; (2) Moses is made to be "a kind of legal fiction," whose prominent role in the Pentateuch is difficult to account for; (3) the authority and credibility of the Bible as a whole are discredited.[3] Assuredly, Mosaic authorship is a well-founded fact.

Title. This fourth book of Moses has had various titles. According to the Hebrew custom of deriving its title from the first word of the inspired Hebrew text, it has been called *Wayyedabber,* meaning "And He said." More generally—and more meaningfully—the fifth Hebrew word has determined a title, *Bemidbar,* meaning "In the wilderness." When the Septuagint translators affixed a title to the book, they chose the Greek word *Arithmoi,* meaning "Numbers," the word being suggested from the two numberings or censuses of the people as recorded in the book (Num. 1 and 26). The Vulgate followed the Septuagint title, using the Latin *Liber Numeri,* "Book of Numbers." The English title *Numbers* was then naturally carried over into the early English versions, and has remained to the present. Other titles have been used, such as the Book of the Journeyings and the Book of the Murmurings, both of which are accurate titles, describing the main account of the book better than the title Numbers. It must be true that not a few readers and students of the Bible have passed by the fourth book of Moses because of the "dry" connotation in its inadequate title.

Relation of Numbers to the Pentateuch

The five books of Moses, as already indicated, constitute a whole. Numbers, as the fourth part of that whole,

[3]Allis, *op. cit.,* pp. 10, 11.

makes its indispensable contribution. This may be seen in the following chart:

MESSAGE ABOUT

	Nation of Israel	*Man*	*God*
Genesis	Birth; infancy	His creation Fall Hope	Sovereignty
Exodus	Delivered from Egypt	Deliverance	Mercy
Leviticus	Given laws of worship	Access to God	Holiness
Numbers	Traveling to Canaan	Conditions for inheritance	Patience
Deuteronomy	Final preparations for entering Canaan	Preparations for new living	Lordship

Geography is the simplest clue to the place of Numbers in the Pentateuch. From west to northeast, broadly speaking, were three major land areas:

EGYPT   SINAI PENINSULA WILDERNESSES   CANAAN

(1) Egypt was the land of bondage for the Israelites, from which they were delivered by God. (This story is found in Exodus 1–14.)

(2) Canaan was the land of promised milk and honey, to which God wanted to lead the Israelites. (Entrance into the promised land is described after the books of the Pentateuch, in Joshua.)

(3) The wildernesses between Egypt and Canaan were the scenes of the testings and judgments of the Israelites on their journey from Egypt to Canaan. (Exodus 15–40 and all of Numbers record the events of these years.)

See the accompanying map for the major geography of Numbers.

The place of Numbers in its contribution to the historical record of the Pentateuch has a direct bearing on the major spiritual lessons to be derived from its message (below).

Broad Survey of Numbers

In the study of any book of the Bible, one should first make a broad survey of the book, looking for such things as highlights, turning points, and emphases. The purpose of this survey is to gain perspective and a fair orientation to the "neighborhood" where the smaller parts of the book will later be located and studied.[4]

Numbers falls logically into three main divisions, easily identified by the geographical location of the Israelites in the account of the book (Moab is the land to the east of the Jordan, the stepping-off place into the promised land):

1:1 10:10	10:11 22:1	22:2 36:13
AT SINAI	TO MOAB	AT MOAB
Preparation for the Journey —few weeks—	The Journey —about 39 years—	At the Gate to the Land —few months—

The following outline describes the work at hand for the Israelites at the above geographical locations:

1:1	10:11	22:2
Order and Organization	Testings and Failures	Repair and Reorganization

Two observations may be made here:

(1) The Israelites at Moab ready to enter the land, with the exception of two people, are a later generation than the ones preparing for the journey at Sinai. This is because God's judgment for sin on the journey was forfeiture of the privilege of entering Canaan.

(2) While the middle section covers a span of about

[4]Irving L. Jensen, *Independent Bible Study* (Chicago: Moody Press, 1963), pp. 106 ff.

thirty-nine years, there is scarcely any record of the events of these years of wanderings. Most of the section deals with events immediately before and after the actual wanderings themselves.

Applying Numbers to Today

After one *observes* what the Bible says, he must *interpret* what it means and then derive its intended *applications*. These three facets constitute Bible study.

The contents of Numbers are approximately half historical and half legislative. The general rules of Biblical interpretation apply equally to both categories. A special kind of Biblical content appears in Numbers—that of types and symbols. Their occurrence is to be expected in a book that describes an era of God's people when He especially used objects, such as the ark and tabernacle, to prophesy of things to come.

Historical Facts. Four major truths learned from historical records in Numbers concern (1) the nature of God, (2) the ways of God, (3) the nature of man, (4) the experience of man. The application of such truths is cited by Paul when he refers to Israel's experiences from Egypt to Canaan: "Now these things happened unto them by way of example; and they were written for our admonition. . . . " (I Cor. 10:11). The timeless universal principles behind the historical facts must always be sought out before applying such an Old Testament passage to the present day.

Exhortations and Commands. Much of Numbers consists of words spoken to Moses or to the people of Israel in the form of legislation. Here again the timeless word must be derived from the word-of-the-occasion if it is to be applied to the present. In some cases, both are identical, as "Remember all the commandments of Jehovah, and do them" (15:39). As the Israelites were always to remember the Word of God, so we are to keep His Word in our hearts today. In other passages, however, such an identical application is not to be made. To the Nazirite who would make a vow to separate himself unto Jehovah was given the specification that he should not "come near to a dead body" (6:6), which act would make him ceremonially unclean. In applying this situation to the present one may say that a Christian who dedicates his life to God, as appealed to in Romans 12:1, 2, must keep his heart and mind purged from unclean things, or things that speak of death and not life.

Major Truths Taught by Numbers

Much can be learned about God from Numbers. *His gracious promise of help* for the Israelites as they drove the enemies out of the land is prominent in the first ten chapters ("Ye shall be saved from your enemies," 10: 9). He who denies miracles will not feel at home in Numbers, where the help of *divine power* is shown to be a necessity in the daily sustenance of at least two million people in a bleak and dry wilderness.[5] *God's unconditional demands* for holiness of life and consecration

---

[5]That there would be at least two million people may be safely assumed according to the following:

603,550	warriors over twenty
+ equal number	all other males
= at least 1 million	total males
+ equal number	total females
= at least 2 million	total population

See C. F. Keil and F. Delitzsch, *The Pentateuch*, Vol. III (Grand Rapids: Wm. B. Eerdmans Publishing Co., 1949), pp. 5-15, and Young, *op. cit.*, pp. 88, 89, for a defense of the two-million-plus population of Israel during the wilderness journeys.

appear throughout the book (see chaps. 5, 6, 18, 30). *His patience and longsuffering,* as well as *His righteous judgments,* stand out noticeably in the section covering the journey, where His people continually murmured and sinned against Him. The *order and organization* which He prescribes for the Israelite hosts in the first and last sections of the book reveal a God who puts no premium on confusion or slovenliness. Many other insights into the nature of God are seen in the story of Numbers.

This book is also a mirror for man to look in. Especially in the middle section of Numbers, from chapters 10 through 21, man's heart is exposed with its many sinful tendencies. The prominent sin of Numbers, in the general category of unbelief and disobedience, is that of murmuring against God. The Israelites no sooner began the journey from Sinai to Canaan than they began to murmur. "And the people were as murmurers, speaking evil in the ears of Jehovah . . ." (11:1). This they did despite everything to their advantage: (1) deliverance from Egypt's bondage; (2) no present problems on the start of the journey; (3) promise of sufficient help from God for the successful arrival in Canaan. (A key verse for Numbers is 10:29: ". . . We are journeying unto the place of which Jehovah said, *I will give it you . . .*")

Further, Numbers has a unique contribution to the life of the Christian when the broad sequence of its historical setting is seen as a parallel situation to Christian living. The writer of the Epistle to the Hebrews makes this significant application, devoting two chapters to it (Heb. 3 and 4). The main thrust appears in this associated set of facts:

(1) God offered the occupation of Canaan to His people Israel.

(2) They failed to enter the land because of unbelief (Heb. 3:19).

(3) Today God offers rest to the Christian, if he will fulfill the conditions of belief and obedience. ("There remaineth therefore a sabbath rest for the people of God," Heb. 4:9.)

The "rest" spoken of in Hebrews cannot refer to heaven, since the epistle teaches it is possible for a Christian to come short of it. ("Let us fear therefore, lest haply, a promise being left of entering into his rest, any one of you should seem to have come short of it," Heb. 4:1). Therefore, this rest is a state of Christian living today, of victory and blessing, where Jesus has preeminence in the heart (hence the fruits of *His* rest), and where the Holy Spirit continually fills the soul. Even as the Israelite needed to watch his life and keep right with God on his journey to Canaan if he would enter the land, so the Christian must "give diligence to enter into that rest" (Heb. 4:11).

Numbers is the story of Israel's *Journey to God's Rest-Land*, the land of Canaan. The Israelites had been delivered from the bondage of Egypt. The land of milk and honey, Canaan, was offered to them. Theirs it would be if they remained obedient to God, and continued to trust in Him.

The Christian likewise has been delivered from the bondage of sin. For his saving faith (not by his works) through the atoning blood of Christ he is assured ultimately of a place in heaven. But now, for this life, God offers the blessings of His rest, in a life abiding fully in Christ. The Christian can enjoy this life now, if he will daily fulfill God's conditions, being approved in the provings and testings which God brings from day to day.

Purposes of the Commentary

In compacting the material of the thirty-six chapters of Numbers into one brief commentary, the author has attempted to preserve and emphasize two things: (1) broad movements in the book, and (2) the most vital facts and teachings, whether specific or general. From these, applications will be suggested from time to time on the basis of the timeless universal principles involved.

It is hoped that through this procedure the reader will gain and maintain accurate bearings through the pages of Numbers; that he will be encouraged to develop an "instinct for the jugular"— an eye for the crucial things; and that an incentive will be born in his heart to look further into this indispensable part of God's written revelation.

Part One

PREPARATION FOR THE JOURNEY

(1:1—10:10)

I. *Order and Organization* (1:1—4:49)

   A. Order of Inventory (1:1-54)
   B. Order of Encampment (2:1-34)
   C. Order of Ministry (3:1—4:49)

II. *Cleansing, Consecration and Final Instructions*
   (5:1—10:10)

   A. Put Out the Unclean (5:1-4)
   B. Judge the Guilty (5:5-31)
   C. Separate Yourselves (6:1-27)
   D. Offer Gifts (7:1-88)
   E. Transition (7:89—8:4)
   F. Cleanse the Levites (8:5-26)
   G. Keep the Passover (9:1-14)
   H. Follow Your Leaders (9:15—10:10)

Part One

PREPARATION FOR THE JOURNEY

(1:1—10:10)

I. ORDER AND ORGANIZATION (1:1—4:49)

THE FIRST PROMINENT TRUTH about the ways of God revealed in the Book of Numbers is His order and planning. This is vividly demonstrated in the Genesis account of the creation of the universe. Here in Numbers it is manifested in His leading a great host of people (at least two million) on a journey through strange lands.

A. *Order of Inventory* (1:1-54)

At this point in the history of the Israelites everything pointed to a goal not yet attained, the occupation of the land of Canaan. This was not the goal of a dreamer, but the goal promised by the God who already had done marvelous miracles in behalf of His very own people. He had formed them into a nation as He had promised Abraham: "I will make of thee a great nation" (Gen. 12:2). He had delivered them from the utmost in human bondage in Egypt. He had also encouraged them as to the reality of occupying Canaan by making prior specific provision for the kind of life and worship which would be theirs. The Book of Leviticus is filled with such provision and direction, e.g., "When ye come into the land which I give you, then shall the land keep a sabbath unto Jehovah" (Lev. 25:2).

Advance day was now imminent for Israel. It was the first day of the second month, in the "second year after they were come out of the land of Egypt" (1:1). The logistic problems of a mass march of more than half a million fighting men, besides the women and children, were of fantastic proportions, exceeded only by the infinite resources of such a leader and sustainer as Jehovah Himself.

The first order of the day in terms of preparation for the journey was that of personnel inventory: "Take ye the sum" (1:2). Moses and Aaron, with the help of princes or heads of each tribe (1:4-16), assembled all the congregation and numbered by tribes every male, twenty years old and upward, able to go forth to war (1:3).

Before even listing the numbers of each tribe, Moses as writer of Numbers was inspired to insert early in the record the fact of his utter obedience to the commandment of God. Moses did not raise doubts about the ultimate outcome of the journey, utter murmurings about the laborious task of census-taking, or push the job over to someone else. The record says, "*As* Jehovah commanded Moses, *so* he numbered them in the wilderness of Sinai" (1:19). If Jehovah's initiative is the first outstanding truth in the opening chapters of Numbers, Moses' obedience is the second.

The count of the men of war begins at 1:20. When all the records were in, this was the count by tribes (apparently recorded in terms of round numbers, rounded off to units of one hundred, except the tribe of Gad): Reuben, 46,500; Simeon, 59,300; Gad, 45,650; Judah, 74,600; Issachar, 54,400; Zebulun, 57,400; Ephraim, 40,500; Manas-

seh, 32,200; Benjamin, 35,400; Dan, 62,700; Asher, 41,500;
Naphtali, 53,400. The grand total was 603,550 fighting
men (1:46).

"But the Levites after the tribe of their fathers were
not numbered among them" (1:47), since their task along
the way would not be to battle the enemy hosts, but to
take care of the tabernacle and its belongings, and to
minister in its services (1:50-53). In the eyes of God,
work, war, and worship were a trio, each part of which
was indispensable to the successful completion of the
journey to Canaan. Even if the success of a battle depended on hosts of men, it would never call away a
Levite from his duties connected with the people's *worship*. If the favor of God depended on worship and communion, then *work* and *war*, in their place and time and
by commandment of God, were indispensables to the
sanctity of the people. What the people of Israel needed
to see so desperately was that the General who was planning the strategy *knew what He was doing*, and that to
disobey *His* orders was to bring doom.

"Take ye the sum" (1:2). The numbering of the men
of war before the journey started was in effect a representative measure of the number of the total people of
God. This people of God, recently delivered from the
bondage of Egypt, brought into Sinaitic covenant relationship, and now anticipating entrance shortly into the
promised land of rest, symbolize some interesting spiritual lessons for the Christian today:

(1) Each child of God in the large Body of Christ is
an individual soul, known by his heavenly Father (for
a total number is the sum of *individual* parts).

(2) Victorious Christian living (the life of rest in God)
is possible only for those already redeemed from the

bondage of sin. (Those numbered in anticipation of the march to Canaan had been delivered from Egypt's bondage.)

(3) The attainment of spiritual rest comes by spiritual warfare and by the prevailing might of God. (The numbering anticipated and served the logistic purposes for the battles to come.)

(4) Being a Christian is not a guarantee of automatic victorious living.

This latter truth reflects one of the most sobering facts of the history of Numbers, namely, that of all those counted in this early census of Numbers, only two actually were to enter the land. "All that were numbered of you . . . shall not come into the land . . . save Caleb the son of Jephunneh, and Joshua the son of Nun" (14:29, 30). The writer to the Hebrews reminds us that the people did not enter the land because of unbelief and disobedience.

B. *Order of Encampment* (2:1-34)

A mass of people, unordered, invites confusion and riot. Jesus honored order when He prepared to feed over five thousand people at one time. He commanded them to "sit down by companies upon the green grass. And they sat down in ranks, by hundreds, and by fifties" (Mark 6:39, 40). How much more the need for order and efficiency with over two million Israelites in the wilderness!

Chapter 2 records the details of the positioning of the tribes while they were encamped and while they were on the march. For *encampment,* the locations were identified by the directions east, south, west and north, with the tabernacle in the very center: "Over against the tent of meeting shall they encamp round about" (2:2). The order for *marching* was identified by the sequence as listed in the account.

1. At the Head of the March, the East Campers (2: 3-9)

   "They shall set forth first" (2:9).

   a. The camp of Judah
   b. Next, the tribe of Issachar
   c. Followed by the tribe of Zebulun
   d. At this point (10:17) the Gershonites and Merarites followed, carrying their burden of the tabernacle structure, so as to have this ready when the Kohathites would arrive with the sacred things (10:21).

2. Followed by the Second Rank, the South Campers (2:10-16)

   a. The camp of Reuben
   b. Next, the tribe of Simeon
   c. Followed by the tribe of Gad

3. Next, the Camp of Levites (2:17)

   They were responsible for everything of the camp and tabernacle except that which was carried earlier by the Gershonites and Merarites. As in encampment, so in march, the Levites were to be centrally located.

4. The First of the Rear Divisions, the West Campers (2:18-24)

   a. The camp of Ephraim
   b. Next, the tribe of Manasseh
   c. Followed by the tribe of Benjamin

5. The Hindmost Marchers, the North Campers (2: 25-31)
   a. The camp of Dan
   b. Next, the tribe of Asher
   c. Lastly, the tribe of Naphtali

Chapter 2 closes with a note concerning the obedience of the children of Israel to the directions of God: "According to all that Jehovah commanded Moses, so they encamped by their standards, and so they set forward, every one by their families . . ." (v. 34).

By finding their designated places and keeping to them, the families of the Israelites were taught some vital lessons preparatory to marching and going to war. They were taught to keep their places, whether in camp or on the move; to recognize their dependency on others for protection on all sides; to keep their eyes on the standards, and to heed the voices of their leaders. They were also taught that both camping and marching were in the divine purposes. The journey to Canaan would involve marching, and it would involve camping. Never would the Israelites reach Canaan if they did not keep moving forward; the demands of moving forward would be hard and long, hence the need of mustering renewed strength at camping time.

Perhaps the most important lesson God was teaching the Israelites in the directions for camping and marching was that He, Jehovah, their Covenant Maker and Covenant Fulfiller, must be central in their lives. The tabernacle was not arbitrarily placed in the center of the camp. It was placed there by divine design to be the crossroads of all daily activity, to be the major focus of attention, to be a continual reminder of the Person who dwelt in the midst of the people and Who was rightfully commanding worship and loyalty.

C. *Order of Ministry* (3:1—4:49)

If the success of the journey to Canaan depended on obedient hearts of the Israelites, then a vital part of the journey's preparation involved caring for those things which would encourage and cultivate true worship and spiritual growth. Chapters 3 and 4 record some of God's directions for this preparation. The contents of the two chapters may be summarized:

1. The Priests, Sons of Aaron (3:1-4)
2. The Levites
   a. Their general service (3:5-10)
   b. Their divine Ordainer (3:11-13)
   c. Their number (one month old and upward) and duties (3:14-39)
   d. Their substitutionary position (3:40-51)
3. Duties of Sons of Levi Amplified; Number of Males, Ages 30-50
   a. Kohath: charge (4:1-20); number: 2,750 (4:34-37)
   b. Gershon: charge (4:21-28); number: 2,630 (4:38-41)
   c. Merari: charge (4:29-33); number: 3,200 (4:42-45)
4. Summary of Census of Levites, Ages 30-50: 8,580 (4:46-49)

Priests and Levites were two different classes of ministers. The Levites ministered to the priests (3:6) mainly in the outward elements of the worship services, while the priests performed the ceremonial exercises of the worship itself. In this segment of chapters 3 and 4 only the first four verses refer to the priests exclusively, while the remainder deals with the Levites.

The first note struck by the author is a somber one indeed. Having identified the four sons of Aaron by name—Nadab, Abihu, Eleazar, and Ithamar—and having emphasized that they were "consecrated to minister" (3:3), the author reached back to an event of the past and recovered it—hideous as it was—to impress upon the reader an inviolable truth concerning sin and service: without exception, *sin destroys service*. Nadab and Abihu died at the hands of Jehovah for doing that which the Lord commanded them not to do. They offered strange fire before Jehovah (see Lev. 10:1 ff.). It was a sin of disobedience and presumption. Three important truths stand out in this prologue to the main contents of chapters 3 and 4:

(1) No sins are left unjudged.

(2) Not even God's servants are exempt from judgment. These were sons "consecrated to minister," and when they died, the number of Aaron's sons was reduced by half!

(3) Generations of tomorrow are affected by service today. "And they had no children" (3:4). No sons to pick up the lost strands! God alone knows the full extent of the loss to the generations that followed.

The next three paragraphs are introduced by the phrase, "And Jehovah spake unto Moses" (3:5, 11, 14). Moses was publicly to assign the Levites to Aaron and his sons, to do the service of the tabernacle (3:5-10). Jehovah emphatically declared that the Levites were really His: "The Levites shall be mine . . . mine they shall be" (3:11-13). Then Moses was commanded to number the Levites, every male from one month old and upward (3:14 ff.). In chapter 4 another census was taken, that of all male Levites from thirty to fifty years old. The latter was the census of all *active* Levites serving in their charges. Just as the other Israelites were numbered for war, so the Levites were numbered for their service in worship.

Jehovah revealed a very close relationship between His sovereign appointment of the Levites to service and His sovereign redemption of the Israelites from bondage (3:40-51). That relationship may be seen from the following:

(1) The number of all first-born sons who had been born between the time of the exodus and the census, thirteen months later, was 22,273 (3:43).[1]

(2) The number of all male Levites one month old and upward, was 22,000 (3:39).

(3) Jehovah made a one-for-one substitution for each of the 22,000. "I have taken the Levites from among the children of Israel instead of [in the place of] all the first-born that opened the womb among the children of Israel" (3:12). For the 273 difference, an equivalence of redemption money was paid to the priests (3:46-51).

This transaction illustrates an important truth concerning the relationship of service to salvation. *Sovereign ap-*

[1]The total number of firstborn sons in a total population of at least two million must have been many times the number 22,273. The 22,273 of 3:43 is a correct number; the problem arises because the extra details and stipulations regarding the numbering are not given in the text. See discussion of Keil and Delitzsch on this problem, and the reasons for deriving the number 22,273 from only the thirteen-month period (*op. cit.*, pp. 8-15). Also see Robert Jamieson, A. R. Fausset, and David Brown, *A Commentary*, Vol. I (Grand Rapids: Wm. B. Eerdmans Publishing Co., 1948), pp. 519-20, for other possible explanations.

*pointment to service is based on sovereign deliverance
from bondage.*

Now in further detail the duties of the families of
Levites are elaborated. The sons of Kohath were to have
charge of the primary objects of the tabernacle, such as
the ark, table, candlestick, and altar (4:4-15; 3:27-32).
The Gershonites' service involved taking care of the large
and heavy tabernacle and tent, the curtains, coverings,
screens and hangings thereof (4:21-28; 3:25, 26). The
sons of Merari were to have charge of the smaller auxil-
iary things, such as boards, bars, pillars, sockets, and pins
(4:29-33; 3:33-37).

The Lord knew the details of the objects used in the
worship service, and He provided for their care by the
ministry of the Levites. They must have been impressed
by the meticulous care which He wanted them to exercise in His work. They must have learned the lesson that
each service is as important as the next. For instance,
what would be the point of the coverings and enclosures
(Gershonites' responsibility) without the contents, such
as ark or laver (Kohathites' responsibility)? Or how
could there be a tabernacle without the boards and bars
(Merarites' responsibility)?

The numbers of those Levites who qualified by age
(thirty to fifty) to serve in the tent of meeting were large:
Kohathites, 2,750; Gershonites, 2,630; and Merarites,
3,200 (4:34-49). We are not told every detail of their
duties, but the wilderness environment most certainly
created a multitude of tasks. And for this work there
was a multitude of workers. The Lord was not short of
workers in *that* day!

In the concluding verses of chapter 4 a vital associa-
tion is made, that of "service" with "burden"—"every one

according to his service, and according to his burden"
(4:49). The Levites were to serve faithfully in days of
encampment, and they were also to be willing to carry
the burdens whenever on the march. To serve and carry
burdens—this is the task of the bondslave of the Lord.

II. CLEANSING, CONSECRATION, AND FINAL INSTRUCTIONS (5:1—10:10)

The first four chapters record the directions which
Jehovah gave Moses regarding preparation for the journey as related especially to the community of the camp
as a whole. In chapter 1 the instruction was, "Count the
warriors of the camp"; in chapter 2, "Arrange the tribes
in the camp"; and in chapters 3 and 4, "Take care of the
tabernacle of the camp."

Now the directions were aimed more at individuals
within the camp.

A. *Put Out the Unclean* (5:1-4)

God had placed the tabernacle in the center of the
camp, to emphasize that the life of the Israelites cen-
tered about Him. Now He stated this fact very explicitly
and clearly, and applied it to the life of the camp:

The fact: I dwell "in the midst" of your camp (5:3).

The application: "Put out of the camp every leper,"
and so forth (5:2).

When the Holy One settles down to dwell, uncleanness
and sin cannot find a home there. There is no room for
joint occupancy. If God is *in the midst*, uncleanness must
be put *out*.

Three cases of uncleanness are cited: the leper, the one
with a running issue, and the one defiled by the dead.

Apart from any hygienic reasons, the directions for such purging reflect the ways of God in speaking to the Israelites. They thought in terms of the concrete and the visible, and so God continually used the visible, the tangible, and the audible to make clear His message. Here was a threefold reminder that God did not want habitual sinners in the camp:

The leper was a picture of the awfulness and ugliness of sin.

The running issue was a reminder of sin unhealed and taking its toll.

Defilement by a dead body was a reminder of the ultimate result of sin, eternal death.

"And the children of Israel did so, and put them out without the camp" (5:4). This was another instance of the Israelites' obedience to Jehovah *before* they began to move on the journey.

B. *Judge the Guilty* (5:5-31)

Having taught the Israelites in a symbolical manner that He and sin cannot dwell together, God now legislated what must be done when actual sin occurred in the camp, or when sin was suspected. The kinds of sin that might be committed were legion. God cited adultery as one example.

First, the Lord stated the truths applicable to any kind of sin (5:5-10): (1) every sin becomes part of God's record: "When . . . any sin"; (2) sin is basically "trespass against Jehovah"; (3) for sin there is guilt: "That soul shall be guilty"; (4) restored fellowship with God comes by confession and recompense (vv. 7-10). The timeless, universal truths about sin are clearly recognizable in these four statements.

The remainder of the chapter deals with the case of a man suspecting his wife of adultery, whether she actually committed the sin or not (5:11-31). She was not taken in such an act, hence no one could witness against her. What was the solution? If she was innocent, how could the husband's suspicion be dispelled? If she was guilty, who could justly declare her so? The procedure which Jehovah directed here made prominent this basic truth concerning all sin: *God knows, and God judges.*

The man was to bring his wife to the priest (5:15), who would then "set the woman *before Jehovah*" (5:18). She was to drink the priest's "water of bitterness" (5:18). If she was innocent of the husband's charge, the water would not harm her (5:19). If she had been defiled with another man, then the water would cause her body to swell and her thigh to fall away, and she would be a curse among her people (5:27).

Many sins would be committed by the Israelites on their journey to Canaan, and many innocent persons would be suspected of sins not committed. There would have to be a firm and clear understanding on the part of the leaders and the people how to insure the workings of God's justice. From the directions by Jehovah for this one example of adultery, the Israelites were clearly taught: (1) sins committed in the body are basically sins of the heart; (2) only God knows the heart; (3) only God can and will give fair judgment. How wonderful a society whose supreme court is God Himself!

C. *Separate Yourselves* (6:1-27)

The Lord had just spoken (chap. 5) of a situation when any Israelite sinned and broke fellowship with God. Now—and what a contrast—He spoke of a situation when any Israelite desired to come into closer fellowship with Him and voluntarily assumed the obligations of a vow.

God is not to be known as One who seeks only to expose and judge sin. He also looks for a man who wants to do His will and live for Him. When an Israelite sinned, God would be there to condemn and judge. But when one believed and obeyed God, God would be there to bless and reward. No better illustration of this is to be found in the book of Numbers than in God's judgment in forbidding the doubting Israelites to enter Canaan and His reward in giving Joshua and Caleb the blessed joy of entrance.

Outline of Chapter 6: The Nazirite Vow

1. The Nazirite Vow Made (vv. 1, 2)
2. Requirements for Living the Vow (vv. 3-12)
3. Ceremonies on Completing the Vow (vv. 13-20)
4. The Vow Reiterated (v. 21)
5. Benediction (vv. 22-27)

The Principle of Separation. In the external details of the Nazirite vow God was again seen to use the external symbols to teach the inner basic spiritual truths to His people. Much of the Old Testament teaching is lost if this fact is forgotten. Obedience to the outward form without obedience in the heart has always been hypocrisy in the eyes of God. In Old Testament days, no less than at any other time, God was after the heart.

The word *Nazirite* is derived from a Hebrew root meaning "to separate." Clearly the Nazirite vow was one of separation. Any Israelite could make the vow, man or woman. It could be taken at any time (6:2). The invitation was not to classes or groups, such as priests or princes, since it was not service that was basically involved but living.

The Nazirite vow involved two basic principles:

(1) *The "separation from" principle* (6:3, 4). Here, the emphasis was not on the things from which the Nazirite was to separate himself. The intention of this part of the vow was not essentially to reaffirm one's desire to separate himself from sin. Rather, there was to be a "separation from" on the basis of priorities and surrenders in life. Eating dried grapes (6:3) was not a sinful act, so refraining from eating dried grapes was not an act *per se* of refraining from sinning. Because the vine products as a whole were classified under luxurious and sumptuous living, therefore the Nazirite would be willing to surrender these temporal niceties for fare of eternal values.

The second part of this vow involved the hair (6:5). The Israelitish custom was to keep the locks of the hair short. The law of the Nazirite was to let the hair grow. Such a sight would be a public, visible sign that the person had taken this vow, that he was foregoing society's dignity and custom of short hair in order to go about with the "diadem of his God upon his head" (Lev. 21:12) as the symbol of strength and vitality (cf. II Sam. 14:25, 26). And if there was ridicule by his neighbors for this visible sign of the vow, he was willing to surrender his popular reputation in favor of divine approbation.

The third part of the vow involved provision for an emergency: coming near a dead body (6:6-12). If such a thing happened, even by accident, the Nazirite would bring upon himself ceremonial uncleanness, and he would "defile the head of his separation" (6:7, 9). For such defilement he forfeited his status as under the vow, and he could be reinstated only after fulfilling specified regulations (6:9-12).

In one sense, all three provisions of the vow were rules of "separation from": separation from vine products, separation from customary cutting of hair, separation from ceremonial uncleanness. In another sense, however, only the first rule was a "separation from"; the second was a public testimony of the separation vow; and the third was ceremonial provision for maintaining the sanctity of the vow.

(2) *The "separation unto" principle.* This was the positive side of the vow, and was its ultimate purpose in the life of the Israelite. If God appealed to the "separation from," it was because He wanted "separation unto." "When either man or woman shall make . . . the vow of a Nazirite, to separate himself unto Jehovah, he shall separate himself from . . . " (6:2, 3).

Throughout the chapter the phrase "unto Jehovah" is repeated (see vv. 2, 5, 6, 7, 8, 14, 17, 21). The emphasis is definitely on "Master control." Jesus gave the same kind of invitation to His disciples and the multitude when He said, "If any man would come after me, let him deny himself, and take up his cross, and follow me" (Mark 8:34). There was the "separation from"—denying self—that there might be the "separation unto"—following Christ.

It must not be interpreted that Jehovah, in spelling out the regulations of the law of separation (6:21), was teaching that intimate devotion with Him comes by legalistic works apart from heart attitude. Since the vow was voluntary, the decision to enter it was from the heart (6:2). The duration of the vow was unspecified (6:4, 6), so the individual himself chose the time period, whether temporary or permanent. A command of God can never be really obeyed without the heart's assent. Further, it is on the basis of this fact that one may conclude that if the heart attitude is one of real desire for "separation unto" the Lord, with undivided loyalty to Him as Master of the life, then the laws of the "separation from" will not be difficult commands to obey.

The Aaronic benediction of 6:22-27 is located in the context very appropriately. All the previous verses speak of the *law* of separation; now shines the *grace* of God's face (6:25). The fact that Aaron and his sons were to pronounce the benediction upon the children of Israel did not make it irrelevant to the Nazirite. If such blessings were promised an Israelite, how much greater measure of such blessing could the Nazirite expect! Looking at it from another angle: if the Israelites really perceived that these blessings were all of grace and none deserved, would not some of them, out of gratitude, choose to take the Nazirite vow to enter this special relationship with Jehovah?

The Lord promised to give *happiness* and *security* (6:24). The Lord would give *grace* and favor (6:25). The Lord would give *peace* of heart (6:26). The blessings of Canaan, God's rest-land, were summed up in this great benediction. These were the things the Israelites could have—on the journey and in the promised land—*if* they would put the Lord's name over their lives (6:27). *IF NOT*—that tragic story is told in most of the remaining chapters of Numbers.

D. *Offer Gifts* (7:1-88)

A real measure of the genuineness of a man's living for God is his liberality in giving of his material wealth back to God for His service. In the life of Israel, God made it clear that He wanted worship to be central—on the journey and in the possessed land. Ministers of the worship service, with their material support, were required. The support must come from each of the tribes, whether living in want, as the wilderness trials might bring, or in plenty, as Canaan was promised to bring. How would the people of Israel respond, whether individually, or represented by their leaders?

The response was very favorable. The time was the day that Moses finished setting up and anointing the tabernacle and its furniture (7:1; cf. Lev. 8:10 ff. for the chronological identification). In a few weeks the Israelites would depart from Sinai on their journey to Canaan. A pressing need existed in connection with the service of the tabernacle: how to transport the tabernacle and all its fixtures. There was no problem with the Kohathites: they were to bear the smaller items (ark, candlestick, etc.) on their shoulders, with the use of poles (7:9). But the burden of the Gershonites was heavy (coverings, curtains, hangings); that of the Merarites heavier still (beams and pillars).

The princes, representing each tribe, were up to the occasion. They brought their "oblation before Jehovah": six covered wagons and twelve oxen (7:3). The Gershonites were given two wagons and four oxen, while the Merarites, because of their larger and heavier burdens, received four wagons and eight oxen (7:4-8). The Kohathites needed no wagon help.

But though the occasion of the offering was the mundane need of transportation, the description of the offering emphasizes its hallowed aspects. The offerings are described by such phrases as: "their oblation before Je-

hovah" (7:3); "presented them before the tabernacle"
(7:3); "offered for the dedication of the altar" (7:10, 11;
cf. 7:84, 88). The gifts were given to *God,* as dedicatory
gifts to His service, and then God assigned the gifts to
the mundane need (7:4-8).

With the wagons and oxen were offered other costly
gifts. Each prince brought the same gifts, and because
so much was involved (e.g., slaying animals for offerings)
the procedure of offering was one tribe's gifts per day.
In the text the listings of the gifts, though identical for
each tribe, are recorded at length in what appears at
first glance to be needless duplication (7:12-83), the intention apparently being to remind the reader that _no
gift to God goes unrecorded in His book_. The total sum
of the gifts is given in 7:84-88.

E. *Transitional Section* (7:89—8:4)

Just as the Nazirite chapter describing the vows of an
Israelite ended with the bright note of God's benediction,
so this gift chapter, describing the offerings of the princes,
ends with the warm note of communication by God.
When Moses approached the Lord in the tent of meeting
"to speak with him," then "he heard the Voice speaking
unto him" (7:89). This was the Lord's response to the
readiness with which the princes gave their support to
His sanctuary.

In another respect, verse 89, together with 8:1-4, can
be seen as introductory to what follows, the cleansing of
the Levites (8:5-26). According to 8:15, the Levites
were to go into the tent of meeting to do its service.
What kind of service would that be? Cold, formalistic
and dead, with no contact with the living God? No, it
would be service in a place where God dwelt and where

He spoke with His people. *Voice* is the key word of 7:89.

Further, what kind of service would the Levites perform? That which brought its worshipers into shades of darkness? That which shed no light on other peoples of the world round about, dwelling in darkness? No, it would be service in a place where there was *light, divine light.* Aaron was given the directions: "When thou settest up the lamps, the seven lamps shall give light in front of the candlestick" (8:2, ASV margin). *Light* is the key word of 8:1-4.

A *Voice* and a *Light*—with these the Israelites could be assured of a successful journey through the wilderness.

F. *Cleanse the Levites* (8:5-26)

Vessels chosen of God to do His service must be clean. The choice of the Levites has already been described in 3:5 ff. Some of the duties of their service are listed in 4:4 ff. Now God gave Moses directions for cleansing and offering them for service: "Thou shalt cleanse them, and offer them" (8:15). They were to be symbolically purified from the *defilement of sin* (8:21): (1) by sprinkling water on them, the water probably coming from the laver in the sanctuary; (2) by shaving off the hair from their bodies; (3) by washing their clothes (8:7). Then they were to be ceremonially atoned for from the *curse of sin* by offering two bullocks: "the one for a sin-offering, and the other for a burnt-offering, unto Jehovah, to make atonement for the Levites" (8:12).

Two vital identifications were made in the course of the ceremony. In the first, the Israelites (probably represented by leaders of each tribe) laid their hands upon the Levites (8:10), presenting them to the Lord as their representatives, to serve Him as living sacrifices. In no way, however, were the people of Israel by this "proxy" procedure exempt from their own individual life responsibilities to the Lord. In the second identification, the Levites laid their hands on the heads of the bullocks (8:12), in effect accepting the slaying of the bullocks as symbolizing their desire to present their own bodies to the Lord as a living sacrifice.

The purification rites and the ceremonial offerings teach the truth that God's servants must be pure in heart and sacrificial in spirit. Now appears the complementary truth that these servants must be undivided in their loyalty (8:14-19). Here is amplified what had been recorded earlier about the Levites' appointment (3:5 ff.), that they were separated "from among the children of Israel"(8: 14) and "wholly given unto" the Lord (8:16).

Next, the Lord's servants must be obedient, ready and quick to follow His directions. No more succinctly could the record reveal the obedience of Moses, Aaron, the Levites and the Israelites than by saying, *"Thus did* Moses, and Aaron, and all the congregation of the children of Israel . . . according unto all that Jehovah commanded . . ." (8:20); and, ". . . the Levites purified themselves . . ." (8:21).

Not unrelated to the context of the previous paragraphs, the listing of the age limits for service as a Levite (8:23-26) teaches another truth about the active service of God, that it demands the utmost and the best in strength and wisdom. Here the age spread is given as twenty-five to fifty years. Earlier the ages of serving sons of Levi were stipulated from thirty to fifty years (4:47). The twenty-fifth to the thirtieth year period probably was a term of internship or probation. Before beginning the formal years of service the Levites underwent many years of training, and after completing active duty, a term of lighter service was maintained (8:25, 26). The service of God, whether in the training, probationary, active or semiretired stage, was vital for the success of God's people on their journey.

G. *Keep the Passover* (9:1-14)

The words of the Lord, "When I see the blood, I will pass over you" (Exod. 12:13), may not have been put to music in that day, but they were surely spoken with an authority and impact whose ring will continue to reverberate throughout the halls of time and into the boundless spaces of eternity. At that first Passover event, the Israelites were given the command to "observe this day throughout your generations by an ordinance for ever" (Exod. 12:17). The memorial Passover was to be an annual feast, the first ceremony of which was to fall on the fourteenth day of the first month, at even (Exod. 12:18). Because it was a memorial feast, its main point was to remind the Israelites of their great deliverance from Egypt's bondage. No wonder, then, that it becomes a meaningful point of record in Numbers. For the people had been so delivered. Would they now remember the Lord and keep the feast?

The date of this celebration of the Passover at Mount Sinai, the fourteenth day of the first month, was prior to the date of the opening words of the book of Numbers, the first day of the second month. Why, then, was the recording of this Passover delayed until this point in Numbers? The answer is to be found in the circumstances around the "little Passover" described in 9:6-14.

The main Passover was the great annual feast. Because it was the people's old covenant gospel of the grace of God speaking to them, through the main symbol of the shed blood, of the Lord's gracious deliverance, it was a fitting national celebration on the eve of departure on the journey from Sinai to Canaan.

But God wanted *all* His people eligible to partake to join in the soul-searching events of the feast. For most of the people, there were no major hindrances. To be sure, the task of administering all the parts of the feast to such a multitude was a staggering one, but one can now see why God directed such order and efficiency and participation by so many servants in the services of the tabernacle. It is possible that at least fifty thousand lambs were required for this feast for its approximately two million participants. It was the priests' task to sprinkle the blood (probably on the altar of burnt offering), assisted in this service by the Levites. This was a task of Herculean proportion, but nonetheless very possible (cf. the sprinkling of the blood of 256,500 lambs upon the altars of the temples in Emperor Nero's time). Whatever the staggering tasks facing the servants of God, His inviolable commandment was, "Let the children of Israel keep the passover in its appointed season" (9:2). And no commandment of God regarding the journey was impossible, even if miraculous help was necessary. With sincere and holy simplicity the record answers, "*And they kept the passover . . . according to all that Jehovah commanded Moses, so did the children of Israel*" (9:5).

But some men found themselves, at the time of the Passover, victims of an unfortunate circumstance. They had defiled themselves by contact with human corpses (see Lev. 19:28 for the violation). The desire of their hearts was to join with their brethren in this great and happy, though solemn, celebration. Their own words reveal this intense desire to participate: "Why are we kept back, that we may not offer the oblation of Jehovah in its appointed season among the children of Israel?" (9:7).

Moses wisely sought an answer from the Lord, and received one. And in that answer is reflected again the intention of the Lord to let *all* His people join in this happy occasion. Though such a man was ceremonially unclean, said the Lord, "yet he shall keep the passover" (9: 10)—but one month later (9:11). The same provision of postponed celebration would also apply to one who was on a distant journey at the regular date of the Passover. But the shirkers among the Israelites (and every society has them) could not postpone their keeping the Passover if they were eligible at the time; in fact, for them not to keep the Passover meant being cut off from the people (9:13).

Finally, God would also include the foreigner sojourning among the Israelites who wanted to keep the Passover, as long as he fulfilled the same requirements of the feast. For there was not to be a double standard; rather, "one statute, both for the sojourner, and for him that is born in the land" (9:14).

It is in the provision for a one-month delay that we can understand the placement of the Passover section here in the account of Numbers. The majority of the Israelites had already participated; now the special cases were brought up; now it could be said that *all* the people were ready for the journey.

H. *Follow Your Leaders* (9:15—10:10)

The Israelite hosts had been numbered, organized, sanctified, given adequate spiritual leadership. They had themselves given gifts and oblations to God, and had celebrated the memorial feast of the Passover. In God's estimate they were now ready for the journey as He gave them one last command: know and follow your leaders.

1. Divine Leaders: Signals of Sight (9:15-23)

If up to this point there was any question in an Israelite's mind as to who was really the captain leading the hosts and planning the strategy, there could be none now. For in a clearly visible, undeniably miraculous way, the caller of the signals, the Captain of the hosts, was identified—the God of creation. The visible object was a miraculous cloud. That the cloud was miraculous is seen by the facts: (1) it never dissipated; (2) it did not move according to normal meteorological functions—it might even tarry in one spot for an indefinite period[2] (9:22); (3) at night it took on the appearance of fire (9:16).

The sequence was not, whenever the Israelites stopped the cloud stopped. Rather, whenever the cloud stopped the Israelites were to stop. The principle was that of leadership and following. If the cloud moved, the Israelites must follow; if the cloud stopped, the Israelites must obey (9:17). The action of the cloud was very explicitly identified with the voice of the Lord as Captain: "At the commandment of Jehovah the children of Israel journeyed, and at the commandment of Jehovah they encamped" (9:18). Again and again in 9:15-23 this point is reiterated. In no other place in Numbers is this em-

[2]The Hebrew *yamin* of 9:22 is translated by the A.V. and A.S.V. as "a year." However, the word is used elsewhere to signify an extended indefinite period of time (see Gen. 4:3; 24:55; 40:4), and this is no doubt its intended meaning.

phasis by repetition even matched. The point must have been clear to the Israelites: follow the signals of God!

2. Human Leaders: Signals of Sound (10:1-10)

Communication and revelation from God, clear as it may be, is often missed by the masses if unaided by God's servants. If there was any possibility of false timing or even intentional disobedience of God's signals by the masses, there was insurance in the provision of faithful and discerning leadership by God's appointed servants, Moses, Aaron, and the sons of Aaron (10:8). To the sons of Aaron was given the task of blowing the two trumpets, not only as a marching signal, but also to announce other functions, as 10:1-10 indicates. Moses no doubt was the one who consulted with the sons of Aaron, to give them the signal for blowing.

When the two trumpets were blown, the congregation was to gather at the door of the tent of meeting (10:3). At the sound of one trumpet, the princes were to gather (10:4). When one alarm-type blast sounded for march, the camps on the east side moved (10:5). On the second such blowing, the camps on the south side moved, and so forth, in the order of march earlier organized (10:6). The trumpets were also to herald going to battle (10:9), and to announce the celebration of feast days (10:10).

Trusting in God and following God's leaders, the Israelites were assured victory: "And ye shall be remembered before Jehovah your God, and ye shall be saved from your enemies" (10:9). Should they take their eyes off the cloud and close their ears to the trumpets, however, they were doomed.

Part Two

THE JOURNEY

(10:11—22:1)

Part Two

THE JOURNEY

(10:11–22:1)

I. SINAI TO KADESH—Unbelief (10:11–14:45)

THE JOURNEY from Sinai to Moab was in three stages, not by God's original design but because of events that transpired along the way. The three stages were: to Kadesh; desert wanderings; from Kadesh to Moab. Unbelief was the people's general state of heart in the first stage; in the second, they were reaping the divine chastening in the desert wildernesses for that unbelief; and in the third stage, a new generation took up the journey once again.

A. *A Good Start* (10:11-36)

Nineteen days after the census was taken (1:1) the cloud moved up from over the tabernacle, to tell Moses and the people of Israel that God's time for their departure had come (10:11). The route taken into the northeast was here anticipated in the record by a reference to Paran (10:12), which actually would be the third stop or station along the way (see 12:16). Kadesh, on the southern border of the promised land, was a major goal on the itinerary, and it was only eleven days' journey away—a measure at least of the relatively short distance which lay between the Israelites and their ultimate goal of Canaan. But distance in miles was one thing, proving in experiences was another.

The order in which the camps took up the march is given in detail (10:14-28), similar to the directions given earlier (chap. 2). Here further description is given as to how and when the different groups of the Levites took their places. The Gershonites and Merarites, transporting the tabernacle, went before the tribes of Reuben, Simeon, and Gad, and then followed the Kohathites carrying the sacred things of the sanctuary (10:17-21). This gave time for the tabernacle to be set up at encampment before the Kohathites brought up the sacred articles (10:21b).

Inserted at this point in the text, to identify the human guide which Moses was permitted to have for the journey, is a conversation Moses had with Hobab before the journey began (10:29-32). Hobab knew this area very well and, while the cloud of the Lord would direct the march and show when to encamp, Moses would need to know where to find such things as springs, oases, and pastures, often hidden in these mountains and valleys. Hence Moses' words were, "forasmuch as thou knowest *how we are to encamp in the wilderness*" (10:31). Hobab balked at first, wanting to go back to his own kindred. Moses reiterated that if Hobab came along, he would receive the same blessings Jehovah promised the Israelites. Apparently Hobab consented to go along, although there is no record of his decision.

The first leg of the journey was three days long (10:33); the resting place was later called Kibroth-hattaavah (11:34, 35; 33:16). Whatever might have been the initial problems, discouragements, or hazards, they are not recorded here. Only three facts enter into this diary-like record of Moses at this point, and their prominence is obvious:

(1) The ark of the covenant went before them (10:33). This was the Israelites' confession and testimony at this time that they wanted to follow the Lord and His word.

(2) The cloud was over them (10:34). This was the Lord's testimony and assurance of His continual presence.

(3) Moses kept praying (10:35, 36). This was the voice of the human leader of two million Israelites, interceding for them and claiming God's promises for the march (10:35) and the encampment (10:36).

B. *First Casualties* (11:1-35)

Whatever hardships had arisen by this time, Moses, in writing Numbers, did not yet identify them. They could have been a host of minor irritations, too small to be mentioned individually. But the sin they brought on was no light matter. This was the sin of murmuring, a sin made up of the two ingredients of unbelief and ingratitude. Unbelief, because the people were beginning to doubt whether God would really fulfill His promises. Ingratitude, for they had already forgotten what a favored people they were and how many blessings were daily coming their way. How soon in the life of a believer do such sins arise!

1. *The First Murmuring* (11:1-3)

The account does not say that Moses heard the people's first murmuring as he did on a later occasion (11:10). But Jehovah heard it and in His righteous anger, without announcement to Moses or the people, sent fire to one end of the camp, devouring possessions but probably not killing people. The people appealed to Moses; Moses prayed; the fire abated. Out of fear and awe over this experience this area of the camp was called *Taberah,* meaning "burning."

2. *The Second Murmuring* (11:4-9)

The Israelites may not have associated the fire at Taberah with their personal murmurings, for there was no announcement by Jehovah of such a connection. At any rate, very soon after, another murmuring rumbled through the camp, spurred on by some of the Egyptians who came out of Egypt with them (11:4). From doorway to doorway of the tents throughout the camps Moses heard the cries of complaint over the diet of manna cakes, made from a seedlike substance which God miraculously sent down to the camp with the dew each night. The Israelites overlooked (but surely would have to admit) the fact that food for two million mouths in the wilderness must be miraculously provided from gracious stores above. They presumed to tell their divine Provider what His gracious provision must taste like: fish, cucumbers, leeks, onions, garlic (11:5). God's food was sweet bread from heaven; they wanted some of the sharp and the sour. How much like the sinful heart of man which, without a nature from above, does not enjoy the taste of the food of God's Word.

The anger of Jehovah was kindled, and would take its toll eventually (11:33). In the meantime, the occasion of the murmuring brought a salutary effect, eventually, on Moses' career. Hearing the murmurings of the masses he was driven to despair (11:10-15). He opened his heart to the Lord and asked why the Lord had brought him into such a dilemma. "Do I have to nurse this kind

of child? Where can I get this food to give them? I
can't bear this load alone, it is too heavy for me. Take
my life; don't let me see my dilemma." Moses was not
complaining about his office, but "would stake his life
for it if God did not relieve him in some way, as office
and life were really one in him."[1]

That Moses' despair was not a sin of murmuring like
his people's is clearly indicated by the Lord's immediate
response, which was not a rebuke but an offer of help.
To alleviate Moses' despair of aloneness under the load,
the Lord asked that seventy elders of Israel be gathered
to Him at the tent of meeting (11:16, 17, 24, 25). The
Lord spoke to the men, apprising them of His need of
them to help Moses. Taking the same Spirit which was
upon Moses, God put it upon them. Even as a flame of
fire increases as it reaches out and embraces further objects, so the Holy Spirit is not diminished by His ex-
tension to others' lives, but rather is made more effective.

The immediate sign of the Spirit so resting upon the
seventy men for their newly appointed work was that
they prophesied (11:25). Furthermore, God's encourage-
ment to Moses that such an empowering of the Spirit
could reach even into the very midst of the camp itself
was seen in the event that followed (11:26-30). Two
men, Eldad and Medad, who had been appointed to
appear before the tent of meeting, for some reason did
not come. Nevertheless, the Spirit rested upon them and
they also prophesied, right where they were, in the camp
itself (11:26). When this was reported to Moses by
Joshua, Moses' reaction, though rebuking Joshua for his
jealousy, was one of elation that two more helpers had
been enlisted. In fact, said he, "Would that all Jehovah's

[1]Keil and Delitzsch, *The Pentateuch,* III, 68.

people were prophets, that Jehovah would put his Spirit upon them!" (11:29).

When Moses was originally told to gather the seventy men before the Lord, he was also told to tell the people to prepare themselves to receive, on the following day, all the flesh that they would ever want to eat (11:18). There would be so much flesh that they would gorge themselves for a month, "until it come out at your nostrils, and it be loathsome unto you" (11:20). To Moses' doubt as to where all this flesh would come from, the Lord's pointed rebuke was, "Is Jehovah's hand waxed short? Now shalt thou see . . ." (11:23). And as Moses and the seventy elders went up into the camp of Israel (11:30), they began to see. The next events were a sequence of miracle upon miracle, explained in no other way:

(1) A miraculous wind (11:31).

(2) Quails from the sea area, probably from the Arabian Gulf to the southeast (11:31).

(3) The quails dropped at the camp (11:31).

(4) The miraculous number of quails (11:31, 32), blown off normal course in their migration, so that the birds flew waist high (three feet) above the surface of the earth. The flight lasted so long that the Israelites stood for two days and a night knocking down the quails. To keep them from spoiling the quails were spread about the camp to dry in the sun (11:32b).

(5) The climactic miracle of judgment, in which God smote a number of the people with a very great plague (11:33). This is the first major decimation of the journeying host.

If the lesson of murmuring was not fully learned in this judgment, the place itself might be a reminder in days to come, for the people called it *Kibroth-hattaavah,* meaning "the graves of greediness."

C. *Rebellion of Two Leaders* (12:1-15)

Temptation had come to the multitude of Israelites, and, for their yielding to it by murmuring against God, they suffered terrible judgment by a deadly plague.

But temptation to sin is no respecter of persons, and now it struck at the very leaders of the host. In murmuring, the people had spoken against Jehovah. Now, in envy, two of the leaders spoke against Moses.

The occasion for the envy was set up by the events of chapter 11. Moses, the supreme leader of the entire host of Israelites, received confirmation from God of this high responsibility when God gave him extra help in the service of the seventy elders to whom He gave the power of the Holy Spirit for their tasks. This would not be agreeable to any leader whose heart was corroding with the acid of jealousy.

Miriam, sister of Moses, was a leader under God as prophetess above all the women of Israel. Aaron, Moses' brother, as high priest was in one sense the spiritual head of the entire nation. Miriam's jealousy was the stronger, for she no doubt instigated the rebellion: (1) her name stands before Aaron's in the record; (2) a feminine verb is used in 12:1 in the original text; (3) it was Miriam who received the most severe judgment at the hand of God. Whatever jealousy was in Aaron's heart was complicated by a weak will; for, just as he had not been able formerly to resist the people's request for a golden calf (Exod. 32), so now he succumbed to the evil suggestions of his sister. But while there were no doubt degrees of guilt involved in this duet of rebellion, both were parties to the same

sin, "And Miriam *and* Aaron spake against Moses"
(12:1).

1. *Accusations* (12:1-3)

The complaint against Moses was double-barreled.
The first part was registered to degrade Moses, by suggesting that he had committed a questionable act: he
had married a Cushite woman (12:1). It was probably
after the death of his first wife, Zipporah, that Moses had
married this Cushite woman, who was either one of the
foreigners saved out of Egypt with the Israelites, or a
daughter of the Cushites dwelling in Arabia. In itself
this marriage would not have been wrong, in light of
God's command which simply forbade the Israelites to
marry the daughters of Canaan (Exod. 34:16). Whatever were the facts, this marriage was not even referred
to by God in the "courtroom" trial (12:5-9). And further,
the fact that this accusation was basically irrelevant to
the next complaint makes its motives highly suspect.

The second part of the complaint was registered to
upgrade Miriam and Aaron by suggesting that Moses was
not sole spokesman for God. "Hath Jehovah indeed
spoken only by Moses? hath he not spoken also by us?"
(12:2). We are not told whether or not Moses heard
the accusation of Miriam and Aaron. The record says
that Jehovah heard it (12:2). Very likely Moses at least
knew about their grumbling, and, because it was a challenge of his humility, he would very likely have refrained
from making an issue of it. This may be part explanation
for the insertion at this place of the encomium, "Now the
man Moses was very meek . . ." (12:3). But while Moses
would not have defended himself, God, who heard the
unjust accusations and who leaves no injustice unre-

quited, hastily sprang to action: "And Jehovah spake suddenly [at once—Berkeley Version] unto Moses" (12: 4).

2. *The Trial and Verdict* (12:5-10)

The courtroom scene took place at the door of the tent of meeting (12:4, 5). The persons at the trial were God as Prosecutor and Judge, Miriam and Aaron as codefendants, and Moses as the court's key witness. The Prosecutor presented His case. He had three points: (1) I revealed Myself to prophets by visions and dreams. (2) I revealed Myself to this witness, Moses My servant, faithfully ministering in My whole congregation, in a more intimate way—mouth to mouth, that is, openly and not in enigmas, so that he could very clearly behold my form. (3) Why then did you not fear to speak against such a servant of Mine as this man Moses?

This last point implied the verdict of guilt, which then brought on the punishment of (1) anger of Jehovah against both Miriam and Aaron (12:9); (2) leprosy inflicted upon Miriam only (12:10). Part of Aaron's punishment was grief of soul over this awful plague put upon his sister, and remorse for sinning against God in this foolishness of envy (12:11, 12).

The gracious, Godlike character of Moses shone out in splendor at this moment as he responded to the plea of Aaron and prayed briefly to God, "Heal her, O God, I beseech thee" (12:13). He addressed God here as *El*, the God of creation, for the appeal was for a creative act which only the God of creation could perform, making living flesh out of that which was dead.

Jehovah's response to Moses' intercession was one of grace and justice (12:14). Grace, in that He promised healing. Justice, in that the formal legal requirements of a solitary waiting period of seven days outside the camp (Lev. 13–14), symbolizing the awfulness and hideousness of sin, would be fulfilled. Miriam was restored, but not until she paid for the sin of haughtiness and envy by the humiliation of being "shut up without the camp"— she who was a prophetess among the people of the camp!

D. *Reconnaissance and Report* (12:16—13:33)

The journey northward resumed when Miriam was brought back into camp, and the next stop after Hazeroth was the wilderness of Paran (12:16), around the city of Kadesh (cf. 13:26). The critical hour of testing for the Israelites was soon at hand, at which time their faith—or lack of it—would be manifested to determine their ultimate destiny.

Chapter 13 reveals very clearly to what extent the destiny of the nation of Israel was steered by the persuasive voices of some of its leaders. How important for God's leaders to lead aright! Chapter 14 shows to what extent that destiny was determined by the choice of the people themselves.

1. *The Spies Chosen* (13:1-16)

As the Israelites moved closer to their target, the journey took on more of the somber color and critical air of a military assault. For so major an issue as this, strategy must be God-planned and God-accomplished.

The people's suggestion's for reconnaissance pleased Moses (Deut. 1:22, 23), and God instructed him: "Send thou men, that they may spy out the land of Canaan" (13:1). God further stipulated that the spies should be leaders, representative of each tribe, and that each tribe should be represented by one man. Since the people themselves must eventually make the decision of assault or retreat, they should be fairly informed by a group representing all the tribes.

The names of the spies are listed (13:4-16); they were not the princes of the tribes identified at Mount Sinai (1:3 ff. and 7:11 ff.). Caleb represented the tribe of Judah (13:6), and Hoshea, the tribe of Ephraim. While Hoshea (literally, "help") was the name on the official register, Joshua (from Jehoshua, literally, "Jehovah-help") was the name given him by Moses (13:16*b*).

2. *The Information Wanted* (13:17-20)

Moses told the spies where to go and what to look for. They were to observe the whole land of Canaan, beginning at the region of the south (Hebrew name is *Negeb*), that large area between the deserts of the Sinai peninsula in the south and the arable lands of Judea in the north. They were to continue on up into the north country, the hill country (13:17). From the actual description of places spied (13:21-23) Moses' directions apparently included going as far north as the Lebanon Mountain range.

Things to be observed were: (1) the land: was it fertile or bleak, wooded or desert? (2) the people: strong or weak, few or many? (3) the cities: temporary camps or permanent fortresses? (13:17-20). The implication given by the situations to be observed was that if the land looked impregnable, the decision of Moses should be to forego assault. The reconnaissance report, while one of its purposes would be to indicate from what direction assault should be made (Deut. 1:22), was intended more to indicate whether assault should be made at all. This was the point of the people's suggesting such a reconnaissance. God chose to use this situation as the terminal test of faith. He knew what the report would be—overwhelmingly fearful from a human standpoint. What God wanted to do was to face the people with the ultimate in the test of their faith: would they move on in faith into the jaws of annihilation?

Lest the spies themselves should become fearful on their undercover expedition and return with a report without having seen much of the land, they were to bring back samples of the fruit of the land as proof of their actual contacts: "And be ye of good courage, and bring of the fruit of the land" (13:20). Another reason for having the spies bring back some of the luscious fruit was to prove to the people that it really was a fruitful land, even as God had described it (hence the spies' reference to the samples, 13:27).

3. *Places Spied* (13:21-24)

Their trip of forty days took them, as directed, from the wilderness of Zin in the south to the entrance of Hamath in the far north. In between, they spied on such places as Hebron, south of what was later named Jerusalem, and the nearby valley of Eshcol (literally "cluster"). From this fruitful valley they brought back samples of grapes (clusters grow even today as large as twelve to twenty pounds), pomegranates, and figs.

4. *Report Given* (13:25-29)

At the end of forty days the spies returned to Moses, Aaron, and the congregation of Israel, who were still waiting for them at Kadesh in the wilderness of Paran. The report was twofold: (1) The land is exquisitely fruit-

ful—look at our samples (13:27). (2) *Howbeit*, the land
is impregnable: the people are strong, the cities are large
and fortified, and the land is overrun with various peoples: Anakites (giants); Amalekites in Negeb; Hittites,
Jebusites, and Amorites in the hill country; Canaanites
by the sea (Mediterranean) and the Jordan River.

The report by the spies was made semiobjectively, but
the men could not help injecting their own pessimism
and defeatism into it. The word "howbeit" (13:28) indicates this. Also, by the time they finished their report, the
people were beginning to catch the spirit of defeatism
and violent objection, so much so that Caleb had to still
the mob (13:30).

5. *Two Opposite Recommendations* (13:30-33)

Caleb's recommendation was to go in and possess the
land. Though Joshua is not cited here as taking sides
with Caleb, shortly the record identifies him with Caleb
(14:6).

The other spies' conclusion was that a conquest of
the land was impossible. Military might against military
might, Canaan was seen to be stronger, especially because of its fortified cities. Even if the Israelites were
able to get into the land eventually, barely squeezing
out the various nations of the land, they would ultimately
in turn be driven out again; for the different nations
would never give up striving for a land of such wealth:
it was "a land that eateth up the inhabitants thereof"
(13:32). Also, man for man, the odds were seen to be
against the Israelites, because in Canaan the spies saw
with their own eyes the Nephilim, who were giants or
supermen. It was simply a matter of a giant against a
grasshopper (13:33). The conclusion of the spies was a

rational one; but because it did not reach a higher level than the human, it was a wrong conclusion.

Caleb, on the other hand, reasoned on the basis of a strong faith in the supernatural. He did not deny seeing the formidable fortifications or the imposing giants. He saw them, but he also remembered what God had earlier promised when the people were still at Sinai. God had said, "And ye shall be remembered before Jehovah your God, and ye shall be saved from your enemies" (10:9). In light of this, Caleb could say, "We are well able to overcome [the land]" (13:30). And then, to wed his conclusion to an exhortation, he appealed, "Let us go up at once, and possess it."

The people were now faced with two opinions. They could not halt between them because the exigencies of wilderness living would forbid that. They must make a choice. Would it be on the basis of a reasonable faith in the perfect word of God, or on the basis of fallible reasoning on the temporal, mundane level?

E. *People's Decision and God's Judgment* (14: 1-45)

1. *Sin of Unbelief and Rejection* (14:1-4)

To a man the congregation of Israel looked on their case as both helpless and hopeless. Wailing by day and weeping by night, they murmured against Moses and Aaron. To go into the land meant one thing: all of them, including their defenseless wives and innocent children, would be murdered by the sword. Better it would be for them to die a natural death, either in Egypt or in the wilderness. In fact, why not go back to Egypt under another captain and die there, if need be (14:3, 4)?

Just as in the report of the unbelieving spies there

was no reference to the promises God had made, so the people said not a word about such promises. They surely knew what God had promised, but their unbelief had vaporized His words away. Their sin was not that of despair or despondency, but of unbelief that God was offering them something good plus the help to get it (cf. Deut. 1:27).

The haughty unbelieving words of the self-sufficient people of these verses were the last words they spoke before they saw the judgment of God beginning to take its toll (14:36 ff.). Until then, the voices were those of Jehovah, Joshua, Caleb, Moses and Aaron.

2. *Last Appeal to the People* (14:5-10)

God's men—Moses and Aaron, Joshua and Caleb—knew the Rubicon had now been crossed by the people. The nation had sealed its doom by voting for retreat. In their distress over the people's unbelief, Moses and Aaron publicly fell on their faces in prayer to God, while Joshua and Caleb rent their clothes in typical mourning fashion. Joshua and Caleb made one last appeal to the people, with the hope of reversing their commitment. Their appeal was clear and to the point: (1) the land is exceedingly good; (2) if Jehovah favors us, He will bring us into the land; (3) He will favor us if we do not rebel against Him nor fear the people of the land. The appeal was unheeded; in fact, it stirred up the people to the frenzy of calling for their death by stoning. But God manifested Himself at such critical moments as these, and now His glory appeared in the tent of meeting, in view of all the hosts of Israel.

3. *First Announcement of Judgment* (14:11, 12)

The moment had arrived for the announcement of God's judgment. Here it was stated succinctly and briefly to Moses; God would speak further details later. The judgment for the unbelieving hosts was death and disinheritance. But the nation would not be wiped out *in toto.* Of Moses God would make even a greater and mightier nation.

4. *Last Appeal to God* (14:13-19)

Under the strain of utter distress over his people's sinful ways, Moses nevertheless remained the calm and importunate intercessor between man and God, in many ways a type of Christ in His intercessory work. The basis of Moses' appeal to God was twofold:

a. Don't let the heathen nations have excuse for denying Your omnipotence. Moses reasoned thus: All nations know that You are dwelling in the midst of Israel. If You kill most of Your people, it will be an admission that You have no alternative because You were "not able to bring this people into the land" (14:16).

b. Manifest Your power to the nation of Israel ("let the power of the Lord be great," 14:17). Moses identified that power as the power to forgive, and the power to judge iniquity (14:18). Moses did not need to appeal for the latter, for the Lord had just pronounced judgment. So Moses interceded for the working of God's power to forgive: "Pardon, I pray thee . . ." (14:19).

5. *Second Announcement of Judgment* (14:20-25)

In His answer to Moses, the Lord did not refer to the first of Moses' appeals. The principle at stake there should have been clear to Moses. God never sacrifices the outworkings of His attributes—here, righteousness and justice—for a reputation. To the second of Moses' appeals, God gave a full answer, saying, "I *have* pardoned" (14:20). But if My glory is to fill the whole earth, My justice cannot be withheld. Therefore, because these people have tempted Me "ten times" and not hearkened to My voice, "they shall not see the land" (14:22, 23). The phrase "ten times" may have been a colloquialism to represent full measure, or the Lord may have had ten actual instances in mind. Of such there were many: (1) at the Red Sea (Exod. 14:11, 12); (2) at Marah (Exod. 15:24); (3) in the wilderness of Sin (Exod. 16:2); (4) at Rephidim (Exod. 17:1, 2); (5) at Horeb (Exod. 32); (6) at Taberah (Num. 11:1); (7) at Kibroth-hattaavah (Num. 11:4 ff.); and now the temptings here at Kadesh.

The first announcement of judgment had been death and disinheritance. Now the further detail had been added that the unbelievers would not get to possess Canaan. Caleb with his seed, however, would be allowed to enter, for he followed the Lord "fully" (14:24).

The problem as to where Moses should now lead the people, with the curse of doom over their heads, was anticipated and answered by the Lord: the people were to be brought into the wilderness in the direction of the Red Sea.

6. *Third Announcement of Judgment* (14:26-35)

Now the Lord told Moses and Aaron what judgment was to be announced to the people. In addition to the judgment already described to Moses, these details were revealed: (1) everyone of the original census (twenty years old and upward) who murmured against Jehovah would die in the wilderness in the course of forty years (each year representing a day the spies were reconnoitering); (2) Caleb and Joshua, as well as the children of the people, would enter Canaan at the end of the forty years.

7. *First Fulfillment of the Judgment* (14:36-38)

As an unmistakable evidence that God's word of judgment would be literally fulfilled, the spies, except Joshua and Caleb, at this moment were struck dead with a plague from the Lord. The leaders of the tribes were struck first! The people were not left with a question as to how to interpret the Lord's words of judgment.

8. *Response of the People* (14:39-45)

The immediate response of the people to the announcement of judgment was great mourning. But mourning would not redeem them now. Next, they confessed their sins, in word if not from the heart. But the hour for confession was gone. At about the same time, in a rash and spiteful spirit they ascended a mountain in preparation for marching forward, and flippantly cried out in effect, "OK, we might as well go where Jehovah told us to go" (14:40). But sin begets sin, and the old sin of unbelieving despair led to the new sin of presumptuous self-confidence. Moses, who had just been warned of God not to advance into the hands of the Amalekites and Canaanites (14:25), passed on this warning to the people (14:42, 43). But they, in their haughty self-confidence, went anyway—without the Lord ("Jehovah is not among you," 14:42), without the ark ("the ark . . . departed not," 14:44), and without Moses. The result was inevitable, and at the hands of the Amalekites and Canaanites the first large contingent of the more than 600,000 warriors was wiped out.

II. DESERT WANDERINGS—Divine Chastening (15:1—19:22)

The next thirty-seven years or more were transitional years in the history of the nation of Israel. (When the commencement and closing days of the wilderness experiences were included, the total time period was forty years.)

The history of Numbers records very few events of these transitional years, for in a real sense they were years of void: one generation of Israel's sacred history was quickly dying off, and its rising youth as yet had no history at all. But though the period lacked in events, it did not lack in its significance as a transitional period.

Geographically, the people neither advanced nor retreated; rather, they wandered aimlessly about the wilderness and desert areas, between Kadesh and the Red Sea (14:25), consuming the years of God's calendar of judgment. Some of the names of the camping places are listed in 33:19-36. When the judgment years came to a close, the nation returned to Kadesh (20:1), ready then to advance toward Canaan.

Populationwise, the thirty-seven years produced the major change. The 600,000 warriors met their appointed death over the space of the years, some by violent causes (16:49), and were buried in the wilderness—daily reminders of the great judgment of God. Children and youth under twenty years of age grew up, were married, and reared children, and by the end of the wandering years a new generation of the seed of Abraham had appeared.

Spiritually, new seeds of hope were sown, the original covenant and promise reaffirmed, and preparation for entering God's land renewed. For this spiritual ministry among the people, God still had His servants Moses, Aaron, Aaron's sons, the Levites, Joshua, and Caleb. The record of Numbers now puts into focus the major spiritual issues of these transitional years.

A. *God's Legislation Reaffirmed* (15:1-41)
1. *By Restatement* (15:1-31)

God saw the need of pointing the new generation in two directions: (1) the promised land ("When ye are come into the land," 15:2), and (2) the law given on Mount Sinai (see the books of Exodus and Leviticus). Lest there be the mistaken notion that the laws of Sinai, including the laws of offerings, had been abrogated or replaced, the Lord explicitly cited some of them again, including the meal, drink, slain and burnt offerings (15:3-10). These offerings stressed the possibility of worshiping God; the way of access to God (substitutionary atonement by blood); the universal invitation to worship God (15:11-16; e.g., "One law and one ordinance shall be for you, and for the stranger that sojourneth with you"). The heave offering (15:17-21) stressed the fact of thanksgiving to God for His providence: "When ye eat of the bread of the land, ye shall offer up a heave-offering unto Jehovah" (15:19). For national sins committed unwittingly, there were offerings (burnt, meal, sin, drink) to bring forgiveness (15:22-26). For sins committed unwittingly by individuals, a sin offering would bring forgiveness (15:27-29).

But, warned Jehovah, the sin of open rebellion against Him, raising one's hand ("with a high hand") against

Him, was a sin of blasphemy and was punishable by death (15:30, 31). This sin is the kind that originates in a heart which despises God's Word, and therefore breaks God's commandments openly and fearlessly. God made it very plain that souls of this sort would not be tolerated in the land of Canaan—nor in any land. The Israelites were to see this demonstrated in the action of the next few verses.

2. *In Demonstration* (15:32-36)

One of the laws of Mount Sinai was, "Whosoever doeth any work on the sabbath day, he shall surely be put to death" (Exod. 31:15; cf. 31:14; 35:2). Here in the wilderness a man was found gathering sticks on the sabbath day. Did the Sinaitic law apply here in the wilderness? The people knew it did, even as they had been taught by God that it would apply also in Canaan. They brought the man to the tribunal—Moses, Aaron and the congregation—who put him in ward until the Lord indicated by what kind of death he should die (15:34), for the Sinaitic law did not supply this detail. God's answer to Moses was: death by stoning by the congregation outside the camp. In obedience, the people did what the Lord instructed. How the law of God must have made an indelible impression upon the hearts of these people through this dreadful experience!

3. *Help for Remembering* (15:37-41)

The stoning of a man was one of God's pedagogical methods of teaching His people the vital truth of obeying His word. The intensity of the minutes of stoning would not easily fade from their minds.

Another way God taught His people His law was by

the frequency of reminder—in the daily physical view of
a fringe on the borders of their garments. The fringe was
actually tassels, placed at the four corners of the upper
garment (Deut. 22:12). The tassel was to be fastened
by a cord of blue. The sole purpose of the tassel was to
be a continual reminder to the Israelites (1) to remember
all the commandments of God, (2) to obey them, (3) to
follow not the way of self, and (4) to live holy unto God
(15:39, 40). For, said Jehovah, "I am Jehovah your God,
who brought you out of the land of Egypt, to be your
God: I am Jehovah your God" (15:41). The universal
timelessness of these exhortations to holy living is obvious.

B. *God's Leaders Challenged* (16:1-50)

The most critical event of the years of wandering was
the rebellion of Korah and his company against Moses
and Aaron. Miriam's and Aaron's envy against Moses
before the pronouncement of judgment at Kadesh was
mild compared to the sedition stirred up by Korah. In
both situations, however, the issue was the same: out of
sheer jealousy, God's leaders were challenged in their
divinely appointed positions. And because they were
God's leaders, the challenge was really against God;
hence Moses' words to Korah, "Therefore thou and all
thy company are gathered together against Jehovah . . ."
(16:11).

The sustenance, rule and guidance of a mass of people
required order of life, respect of authority, and organization of functions within the total community. Without
these, chaos was inevitable. For this reason the record
of Numbers has so much to say about them.

The Israelites did not lack those who aspired to be

leaders. In fact, this was their problem. For success, yea, for survival itself, their leaders must be of God's appointment. Korah and his cohorts presumed to challenge God's sovereign choices.

1. *The Challenge* (16:1-3)

The rebels are identified as Korah, a Levite, the leader; Dathan, Abiram, and On, Reubenites (On's name drops out of the story; apparently he was not a prominent leader in the protest); and two hundred and fifty princes of the congregation, men of renown. They charged Moses and Aaron with retaining their top positions ("above the assembly," 16:3) when there was no need of their leadership any more: "It is enough for you" (16:3, margin). (Really, Korah's intention was not to dissolve the offices, but to replace the officers.) Their justification for claiming that spiritual leadership was not needed any more was that (1) all the congregation were holy, "every one of them" (16:3), and (2) Jehovah was in their midst. The latter statement was an accurate one; in fact, it was to be demonstrated shortly when this same Jehovah, dwelling in their midst, would identify sin and consume the sinners, Korah and his company. The former justification was a false one, as the events of the next day would show when God would consume "in a moment" those whom Korah called holy (16:21).

2. *Moses' Response and the Test* (16:4-17)

Though he was Israel's top leader, Moses recognized those occasions where it was the part of wisdom to let God reveal His mind directly to the people without using him as the spokesman. This was one of those occasions. "Jehovah will show who are his, and who is holy" (16:5).

The time of the public demonstration whereby God would make that identification was set for the morrow. Korah and his company were to bring their censers with burning incense before the Lord at the door of the tent of meeting. At that time God would show who were His holy servants.

After setting up the appointment, Moses exposed the real root of trouble in the hearts of the rebels. The sons of Levi belittled their own calling to service, and desired with envious eye the position of the priesthood (16:9, 10). They disregarded the fact that theirs also was a high calling, involving (1) separation by God, (2) closeness to Him, (3) service of His tabernacle, (4) ministry to His people (16:9).

Moses was further challenged by Dathan and Abiram, whose complaint was that not only had Moses taken the people away from a fruitful land (Egypt) and failed to bring them into the promised land flowing with milk and honey (Canaan) but in all this he had made himself a prince over everybody (16:13). This incited Moses to a rare moment of wrath, when he asked God to refuse their offering (16:15), and reiterated to Korah the arrangements for the following day's test before Jehovah (16: 16, 17).

3. *The Day of Reckoning* (16:18-40)

The events of the day of reckoning unfolded with precise timing and without question as to who was master of the day. It was the One whose glory appeared to all the congregation as the rebels gathered the people to their side at the door of the tabernacle, in the presence of Moses and Aaron. God told Moses and Aaron to remove themselves from the congregation, for He would consume the people in a moment. Because of the plea of Moses and Aaron to spare the people, since Korah was the real instigator of the sedition, God gave the people another chance, and they were permitted to move away from the tents of Korah, Dathan, and Abiram (16:24, 26).

The critical moment had arrived. Moses spoke. If Jehovah had not chosen Moses to this position of leadership, Korah and his company would, in the natural course of events, eventually die the common death of man. But if these men had despised Jehovah (16:30), the sign of Jehovah would be the creation of a sudden catastrophic situation: the ground would "open its mouth, and swallow them up" (16:30). At this moment God, who spoke before by word, now spoke by action, and the earth swallowed up the men, together with Korah's servants and all their goods (16:31-33). In terror, the people fled, while the two hundred and fifty rebel princes, holding censers in their hands, were devoured with fire from Jehovah. Since the brazen censers held by the men were holy vessels, Eleazer, son of Aaron, was instructed to recover them from the burning cinders and to beat them out for a covering of the altar, as a continual reminder to Israel of what happens when one who despises God stands in His presence (16:36-40).

4. *Further Consequences* (16:41-50)

But those spared the judgment of one day hastened to sin on the next. As one mad mob the congregation charged Moses and Aaron with murdering God's princes. At that very moment they saw God's cloud covering the tent of meeting in what must have been an unusually awesome sight, attended by the glory of God. Moses and Aaron, warned by God to move away from the congregation while Jehovah would consume the people, hastened to bring an offering of incense as atonement for the people. But the plague had already begun, so that by the time Aaron brought the incense, he was standing "between the dead and the living" (16:48). The toll was 14,700. The judgment of the years of wandering continued in its sure fulfillment.

One wonders what was in the hearts of the people who were spared this last dreadful plague. They knew they were not spared because of faithful hearts or repentant ones. They should have been convinced, by the timing of the cessation of the sudden death plague with the atonement offering, that what saved them was the quick action of Moses and the faithful intercession by the high priest of God through an offering of the sanctuary. The very ones whom they called murderers had proved to be their "saviors." No better approbation by God of His leaders could have been manifested to the people.

C. *God's High Priest Vindicated* (17:1-13)

In still another way God would prove to Israel that the leaders of the congregation were His appointees. A situation was set up for a visible sign of God's unmistakable vindication of Aaron as high priest, and also of God's disapproval of the people's murmuring.

1. *Presentation of the Rods* (17:1-7)

Again, according to the usual revelatory procedure of this period, the directions came from God to Moses. Each tribe was to be represented by one rod or branch of an almond tree, upon which was to be inscribed the name of the tribe. Since the number of rods was twelve (17:6), and since one rod was for the tribe of Levi, with

Aaron's name on it, very likely Ephraim and Manasseh were represented as the one tribe of Joseph (cf. Deut. 27:12). The rod symbolized a man's rule over his house. In the case of a prince, it was in effect his scepter of authority. For the rods of the twelve tribes, therefore, the significance of the forthcoming action would relate to this aspect of rule and authority.

All twelve rods were to be laid in the tabernacle before the ark of the covenant. In the appointed time, the rod of the man of God's choosing would bud, and this sign was to settle once and for all ("make to cease," literally "bring to rest") the questionings and murmurings over who was God's man (17:5).

2. Budding of Aaron's Rod (17:8-11)

The next day brought the answer. When Moses entered the tabernacle, he saw that it was Aaron's rod that had budded. Moses doubtless anticipated that Aaron would be God's choice, but what must have been an unexpected sight to him was to see blossoms and ripe almonds on the rod, in addition to buds. This surely must have spoken an additional message to him and to all the people concerning the ministry of the priesthood and the man filling the office. This was a ministry designed of God to bear eternal fruit. Only a man empowered by the Spirit of God could serve effectively in such a ministry. Aaron, said God through this symbolic action, was such a man.

The other eleven rods were returned to the tribes, who, as "they looked" (17:9) and saw no bud on theirs, must have had sobering thoughts of introspection. God did not intend thereby to humiliate the heads of the tribes but to show all the people anew that each man must fill God's place for him and not seek some other position. Aaron's rod was to be kept before the ark as a reminder of the sin and folly of the people's rebellion against God's leaders.

3. *The Effect* (17:12, 13)

The effect on the people was not one of reviving any faith on their part, but nonetheless the effect was salutary. For they were brought to that place of utter helplessness and of being undone which, if directed aright, would lead to faith again. "Behold, we perish, we are undone, we are all undone," their voices cried out in crescendo. They now saw themselves as those who could not compete against God: "Every one that cometh near unto the tabernacle of Jehovah dieth" (17:13). Quite a contrast to the bold challenge made earlier against God and His servants!

D. *God's Priests and Levites Provided For* (18:1-32)

When the Israelites would finally enter Canaan and appropriate the land and its fruit for a perpetual inheritance, there would have to be an understanding as to what lot and provision fell to those serving in the things of God's sanctuary, since they would own no land to produce a living. What would their inheritance be? It was at this point in the experiences of the Israelites that God revealed His plans for them, as He spoke through Aaron (18:1-24) and Moses (18:25-32).

A key phrase of this chapter is "I give you" (18:7; cf. vv. 12, 19, 26, etc.). God takes care of His own. If He promised to give a rich land to the multitude of His people, He would also give good things to the chosen serv-

Numbers

ants of His house. Observe the following references to gifts.

First, the very office of priesthood was a gift of grace. This was cited by God later in His words to Aaron: "You and your sons are to discharge your priestly duties in everything, from that which pertains to the altar to that which is inside the veil. Be sure to perform it, for the office of the priesthood is a gift which I am giving you" (18:7, Berkeley Version). The office was said to have the character of a gift, evidently because the priest's intimate fellowship with God was a privilege accorded not for works done, but wholly by the grace of God.

Second, God gave His ministers a spirit of responsibility for the critical task to which they had been called. The priests Aaron and his sons, together with those of his father's house (of the family of Kohathites), were bearing the iniquity of the sanctuary and of their own priesthood (18:1). If there was atonement for any sin or defilement whatever—whether in the gifts or offerings themselves, in the people, in the priests, or in the Levites —that atonement applied only as the priests faithfully discharged their duties. The ultimate work of the priests was "that there be wrath no more upon the children of Israel" (18:5).

Third, God gave His ministers the gift of helpers. Concerning the Levites taken from the children of Israel (chaps. 3 and 4), God said to the priests, "To you they are a gift . . . to do the service of the tent of meeting" (18:6). The phrase "joined unto thee" (18:2) indicates that the Levites were intimate helpers and were to serve the priests in their charges.

Fourth, God gave His ministers every provision for earthly needs. Since the priests and Levites would not

be receiving land in Canaan from which to draw a liveli-
hood, other than that of the Levite cities (see chap. 35),
God designated that their income should be taken from
the gifts and offerings brought to God in the sanctuary
(18:8-32). Verse 8 identifies in general the source of income: "I have given thee the charge [keeping] of my
heave-offerings," the phrase "heave-offerings" being used
here to include all the holy gifts brought to God in the
offerings. This is borne out in the words of God which
followed, identifying such gifts: meal offerings, sin offerings, trespass offerings, oil, vintage, grain, fruits, everything placed under a ban (18:14; cf. Lev. 27:28), and
the firstborn of man and beast, the former being redeemed by money. The Levites, on the other hand, were
to receive as their reward for service all the tithe of the
land which the Israelites were to give to God according
to the regulations described by Leviticus 27:30-33. Of
this tithe, the Levites were to return a tenth to the Lord
(Num. 18:25-32) as their offering to God.

Last, God gave the gift of Himself to His ministers.
This was the greatest of all His gifts. In fact, God's ar-
rangement with the priests and Levites was such that
they would be continually reminded of this. They were
not to receive an inheritance of any portion of the land
of Canaan, because their special portion was God Himself: "I am thy portion and thine inheritance among the
children of Israel" (18:20). And since it was true that in
one sense God was the spiritual portion of the people
as well, it must be interpreted here that there were
unique blessings of fellowship with God afforded His
ministers which the people could not share. The people's immediate dependence for provision was on the
soil; the priests' and Levites' immediate dependence was

on the effective functioning of worship in God's sanctuary (for if there were no worshipers, there would be no gifts and tithes). Stated another way, "the worship (*cultus*) of Him is infinitely fuller of delight, and far more productive, than the cultivation (*cultus*) of any soil."[2]

[2]Keil and Delitzsch, *op cit.*, p. 118.

E. *God's People Offered Cleansing for Mass Defilement* (19:1-22)

The section of Numbers having to do with the years of desert wanderings (15:1—19:22) opens with a reaffirmation of God's laws which would still apply to the Israelites when they reached Canaan (chap. 15). The next three chapters (16—18) reaffirm God's need and choice of spiritual leaders, especially with reference to the service of the holy sanctuary. But all this time the race had been dying away, sometimes falling like flies, as in the case of the more than 14,700 who reaped the sudden judgment of God after Korah's rebellion. Masses of dead bodies, whether dying from plague, war, or natural causes, were a common sight to the Israelites in their aimless desert wanderings. If the law as prescribed by Numbers 5:2-4 was to be fulfilled—and it had to be—the majority of the survivors, for the inevitable frequent defilement because of proximity to dead bodies, would find themselves more often outside the fellowship of the camp than inside. God was especially concerned now with the preservation and spiritual nurture of the rising generation who had not fallen under God's judgment at Kadesh and who would soon be entering the promised land. Hence this new provision of cleansing—which also would remain as a "statute for ever" (19:10)

—was the answer to the problem of the excessive presence of corpses, because of its easier and more efficient application.

1. *Preparation of the Water-for-Impurity* (19:1-10)

The basic ingredients of the cleansing agent were to answer to the basic problem of the Israelite involved. He had come near or had touched the dead body of a man, and for this he was legally declared defiled or unclean (19:11). For the death aspect, symbols like the color red (red speaking of the intensive flush of life, as blood is red) determined one constituent of the cleansing agent. For the defilement aspect, the symbol of water (cleansing being one of its major uses) determined another major constituent. The following list of additional ingredients, or actions, suggests other symbolical intentions of the cleansing solution: "heifer," a female animal, the female being the bearer of life; "without spot . . . no blemish," emphasizing purity; "sprinkle her blood" for atonement for the sin of defilement; "burn the heifer" —everything burned, in the fire of purging; "cedar wood," a symbol of incorruptible continuance of life; "hyssop," symbolizing purging; "scarlet [wool]," to intensify the red color of the ashes as a symbol of life and energy. When all the ingredients were burned, the ashes, representing the unconsumable, were mixed with water in a vessel when ready to be applied (19:17), and this then became the "holy alkali" of purification.

2. *Cases Needing the Water-for-Impurity* (19:11-16)

A man became defiled in any of these situations: (1) touching a dead body of any man, including one slain by the sword on the battlefield (19:11, 16); (2) touching a bone or grave of a dead man (19:16); (3) being present in the tent where a dead body lay (19:14). (Any open vessel in the tent also became defiled.) The defilement lasted for seven days, at the end of which (1) the man was accepted as clean if he applied the purifying water on the third and seventh days, or (2) the man was doomed to die for his defilement if he failed to apply the water (19:13).

3. *Procedure for Application* (19:17-22)

Any clean person could apply the purifying water on the unclean. On the third day he was to take hyssop, dip it in the water, and sprinkle the water upon the defiled man, and upon any vessels, or even the tent, if they also had been defiled. The sprinkling was repeated on the seventh day, at which time he that had been defiled was to wash his clothes, bathe himself, and by evening he was clean again.

✿   ✿   ✿

Before long the people were to move out of the desert on their march toward the promised land. One thing they could not leave in the desert but had to take with them even into Canaan was the inviolable law of natural death. Legal defilement by contact with dead bodies, and the ceremonies of purification required, would be continual reminders to them that God would give the Canaan blessings only to those who were clean.

The Christian today who would covet the blessings of "rest" in Christian living, of which the author of Hebrews speaks, must also see that such blessings come only to the undefiled, to those whose sins have been confessed and to whom the cleansing blood of Christ and purging Word of God have been applied and obeyed.

III. KADESH TO MOAB—A New Generation and a New Start (20:1—22:1)

Almost forty years of wilderness wanderings had now been experienced. In the first month of the fortieth year from the commencement of the wanderings—the exodus from Egypt—the people returned to the wilderness of Zin, the region around Kadesh (as to the time, see 14:32 ff.; 20:1 and 33:38). The time for a new start had arrived. The old generation under judgment had passed away; the new was ready to march. This section of Numbers recording the events from Kadesh to Moab (20:1—22:1), reflects a changed situation and reveals all the anticipations of actual conquest of the promised land of Canaan. Chapter 20 gives the first specifics of the retiring of the aged but faithful leaders, while chapter 21 records the first set of new battle victories and marching advances.

A. *First Signs of Retiring Leadership* (20:1-29)

1. *Death of Miriam* (20:1)

While the people dwelt at Kadesh waiting for instructions to march, Miriam the prophetess died, and was buried there. Nothing is said of the cause, the occasion, or the effect of her death. This strikes one as being a notable omission, especially since the deaths recorded for the previous years were usually associated with sin as a cause, violence as the manner of dying, and some intense reaction as the sequel. But none of these things are attached to the story of Miriam. It is significant that the record of the natural death of a prophetess of God should appear after the conclusion of a morbid era of judgment and at the commencement of a new and promising experience for the people of God.

2. *Moses and Aaron Fail at Meribah* (20:2-13)

The test of leaders is in the discharge of their duties. Their main duty is the leading of the followers. Followers, then, are the testing grounds of the leaders. This was the case here. The people, again without water, murmured against Moses and Aaron, wishing they had died earlier with their brethren. This was a test of Moses' and Aaron's patience—how many times had they not heard this cry? It was a test of their love—could they rebuke the parched tongues of mothers and children, or even of complaining fathers? Above all, it was a test of their faith—would they count on God once more to show Himself Lord of creation and Lord of His people at one and the same time?

Their first reaction was the usual one; they fell on their faces, knowing full well that this murmuring would anger the Lord. But at this moment the Lord appeared in His glory and instructed Moses to take the rod which was before Jehovah, the rod with which Moses had performed miracles in Egypt (Exod. 17:5), and in the presence of the people and Aaron to command the rock, which was in full view, to bring forth water. In obedience, Moses took the rod and gathered the assembly.

But within the hearts of Moses and Aaron the weight of impatience and unbelief, even rebellion, had been pressing harder and harder, and now the breaking point had come. First was the quick temper of unkindness in how Moses addressed the people, "Hear now, ye rebels" (20:10). Then came glorification of self by emphasizing the "we" and not saying a word about Jehovah: "Shall *we* bring you forth water out of this rock?" Finally follows the outright act of disobedience of God's instructions. God had said, "Speak ye unto the rock" (20:8); Moses instead smote the rock twice with his rod (20:11).

God gave the people and the cattle the water they needed, but He also gave Moses and Aaron the rebuke which they deserved. He identified their sin as unbelief and failing to glorify Him in holiness before the people (20:12). The penalty He announced was heavy but just: forfeiture of the privilege of leading the people into Canaan (20:12). The people would enter the land, but Moses and Aaron would not be with them. This must have been a sad moment of judgment for Moses and Aaron. In the story of Numbers it is the place where the human hero gives way to the real hero of the story, God himself.

When leaders fail, God's holiness and might and glory are not marred. This is the story of Meribah (meaning "strife"). When the people strove against God, God showed Himself mightier. When the leaders failed to give Him glory and to reveal Him as the Holy One of Israel, He manifested Himself both in the miracle and the judgment. No water for the congregation (20:2) became the occasion for His being "sanctified in them" (20:13).

3. *Moses' Envoys Fail in Negotiation* (20:14-21)

This is the first record in Numbers of a plan of march at the end of the forty years of journeyings. The easiest route to Canaan for two million people was not due north from Kadesh through the treacherous hills and mountains of Canaan, a route where they would be exposed to the waiting armies of defenders. Rather, as a topographical map of Palestine indicates, the line of march crossed the low plains of the Arabah which lie south of the Dead Sea, then proceeded northward along the east side of the Dead Sea on the plateau level, and finally reached the plains of the Jordan opposite Jericho, where preparation would be made for the final thrust into Canaan proper.

Moses desired to obtain peaceful right-of-way from the rulers of the lands through which Israel had to travel. The land of Edom was the first of them. It lay to the east of the wilderness of Zin and south of Moab, occupying most of the Arabah. Because of its king's highway (20:17) running north-south, the journey to Moab would have been comparatively easy through Edom. Moses sent envoys to its king to request passage rights, which were promptly denied. This would have been a blow to the spirits of any leader, for were not the Israelites now to expect divine favor on their journey to Canaan? And was not Moses' offer to Edom a very considerate one? No marching through their fields and vineyards, no drinking of their water without paying for it, no detours along the way (20:17-19). Though the negotiations failed, Moses, so recently rebuked by Jehovah in severe judgment, showed the leadership he had formerly displayed, so that when Edom refused to give passage Israel merely "turned away from him" (20:21), that is, looked for another way.

4. *Aaron Dies* (20:22-29; see also 33:38, 39)

When the Israelites reached Mount Hor, which was situated near Edom's border, God told Moses and Aaron that Aaron's day of gathering unto his people had come, and that he would die there on the mount (20:24-26). His garments were to be placed on his eldest son, Eleazar, who would be the new high priest. At the top of the mount the transfer of garments was made, and Aaron, age 123, died.

When the people learned of his death, everyone "wept for Aaron thirty days" (20:29). Theirs was the experi- ence which God's people centuries later would not have to suffer. Their high priests over the years were "many in number, because that by death they are hindered from continuing" (Heb. 7:23). The Christian would have but one high priest, Christ, who, "because he abideth forever, hath his priesthood unchangeable," ever living to make intercession (Heb. 7:24, 25).

So ends the dark chapter. In it has been recorded the death of a prophetess, the critical sin of Moses and Aaron, the refusal of negotiation, the death of Aaron, and the mourning of the people. The chapter has emphasized the limitations of man—even God's leaders! Now with a brighter spotlight on the grace and glory of God, Num- bers resumes its story of advance.

B. *Successful Advances to the Plains of Moab* (21:1—22:1)

1. *Against the King of Arad* (21:1-3)

Some have placed these verses chronologically after the first clause of 20:22. Others interpret 21:1, 2 to refer to a prewilderness vow, and 21:3 to God's postwilderness response. However, the sequence of chapter 33, which is a chronological sequence, retains the same order as that of this chapter, implying therefore that the events of this paragraph happened here, contemporaneous one with the other (see 33:40).

The order of battle was clearly of divine plan. The king of Arad, dwelling in the Negeb region, captured some Israelites in a token war. The Israelites asked God

for help. God heard, and delivered the Canaanites into
Israel's hand, the Canaanites and their cities being utterly
consumed. The experience had three salutary effects:
(1) in one sense it was a retaliation by Israel-in-belief for
a defeat against Israel-in-unbelief (14:45); (2) it was
an encouraging token by God of His favor toward Israel
now in their pursuit of Canaan; (3) it would circulate a
reputation of strength for Israel among the Canaanites in
preparation for the future battles of Joshua against those
nations.

2. *With a Brazen Serpent* (21:4-9)

The hindrance and foe of discouragement and murmuring reared up again, this time at a most untimely moment,
as the people were actually on the march. They had left
Mount Hor and were intending to "compass the land of
Edom" (21:4), whether on the east or west side is difficult to determine. They had no bread or water, and
loathed the manna. For their speaking against God and
against Moses, judgment fell by a scourge of "fiery serpents" which fatally bit many of the people. The general
area of this scourge is known even to the present day
for its many venomous reptiles. Through this plague
God was reiterating the unchanging and universal truth
that sin brings judgment, whether committed in this era
or that. The fact of God's presence on the march gave
no license to commit the old sins of the wilderness. At
the confession of the frightened people and the intercession of a faithful Moses, God set up a condition for
the people's deliverance. A brass fiery-looking serpent
was to be made and set high on a standard. When some-

one was bitten by a live serpent, he was spared death by looking upon the brazen serpent.

It is a known fact that common to most if not all heathen religions of antiquity in these lands was the belief that the serpent had health-giving and healing power and was therefore worthy of worship. Hence the making of statues and objects in the form of serpents, which were appealed to for help in the heathen worship practices. The brazen serpent which Moses was commanded to raise on a standard had no allusion whatever to the heathen practice. The object chosen was a serpent statue because it was to correspond to the deadly serpent scourge that had come to the people. It was cold and lifeless, to represent what God was able to do for the Israelite, i.e., take a fatal, hot sting and render it harmless. Also, it was set upon a pole, to be a visible sign to the people. And finally, its efficacy reached out only to those who would look upon it. The object itself was not to be worshiped. In fact, when the Israelites later began to regard it as an object of worship, it had to be destroyed by Hezekiah (II Kings 18:4).

In this great Old Testament type of salvation-by-faith in a Saviour who died on a cross, the brazen serpent was not a medium for mass deliverance as such. Everyone was not automatically given an antibiotic for the fatal venom of the serpent. Deliverance came only to the *individual* who looked up at the representative symbol. The heresy of universalism is exposed here. Christ, who was in the *form* of sinful flesh, and yet without sin, was set up publicly on the standard of a cross, a visible sign to all the world of the guilt He was bearing. He died as a representative of the race of sinners, and only that individual who looks up to Him in faith is saved (John 3:14).

So the scourge of serpents was a critical experience for the Israelites on the renewed march to Canaan. Were it not for God's grace in granting this miraculous way of deliverance from the very judgment for sin which He Himself was bringing, and the people's individual faith, the march would have ended here.

3. *To Mount Pisgah in Unhindered March* (21:10-20)

The record of these verses takes on the atmosphere of swift advance (though the miles-per-day speed could not have been swift). This is a very obvious change of pace from the earlier movements of the people, when there were stalls, retreats, circlings, obstacles and breakdowns. Now the record begins to read: "And they journeyed from . . . and encamped at. . . ." The succession of places recorded here in Numbers runs from Oboth (21:10); along the valley of Zered, which flows into the southeastern tip of the Dead Sea (21:12); to the other side of the Arnon River, which flows into the mideastern shore of the Dead Sea (21:13); and eventually to the top of Pisgah in Moab (21:20). (See 33:41 ff. for another list of stations on the march.)

4. *Farther North in Successive Conquests* (21:21–22:1)

Moses and his hosts had now reached an obstacle: the land of the Amorites, whose king was Sihon. The experience with this king and his warriors would have far-reaching salutary effects for the Israelites. For God promised to give them this land in battle, and from that day, said Jehovah, "will I begin to put the dread of thee and the fear of thee upon the peoples that are under the whole heaven, who shall hear the report of thee, and shall tremble, and be in anguish because of thee" (Deut. 2:25). Moses asked King Sihon for passage rights, though Moses knew he would be refused. Sihon, refusing Moses, gathered his hosts and fought against Israel at Jahaz. Israel conquered, and possessed the land from the Arnon River to the Jabbok River (the latter flows into the Jordan from the east at a place about one third the distance from the Dead Sea to the Sea of Galilee). This was the land of the Amorites, and at its eastern border was the land of Ammon.

In addition, God gave the Israelites at this time land still farther north, the land of Bashan ruled by King Og (21:33-35), after the crucial battle at Edrei. The Israelites conquered Og and his forces, and "possessed his land" (21:35).

*   *   *

Into this account of the successful journeys and battles of the Israelites, Moses in writing Numbers inserted three songs or poems (21:14-15, 17-18, 27-30). The very fact that the historical events found a place in the work of the poets of the day—the latter two poems being victory verses—serves to illustrate the zeal and expectation of the nation as it reached these points and began to taste victory and blessing instead of the former defeats and judgments.

Now in the plains of Moab (22:1 serves here as a concluding and summary verse for the preceding section), scattered over a large area of encampment opposite Jericho, a great host of men, with their wives, children and cattle, awaited further orders before crossing the Jordan into the promised land.

The instructions they received, and the experiences they had during these transitional days are recorded in the remaining chapters of Numbers.

Part Three

AT THE GATE TO THE LAND

(22:2—36:13)

I. Problems (22:2—25:18)
   A. Opposition from Without (22:2—24:25)
   B. Opposition from Within (25:1-18)

II. Preparation (26:1—30:16)
   A. New Census Taken—Organization (26:1—27:11)
   B. New Leader Identified—Leadership (27:12-23)
   C. Law of God Finalized—Spiritual Life (28:1—30:16

III. Transjordan Business (31:1—32:42)
   A. Decimation of Midianites (31:1-54)
   B. Allotment of Transjordan Land (32:1-42)

IV. Recapitulation (33:1-49)

V. Anticipation (33:50—36:13)
   A. The Task at Hand (33:50-56)
   B. Allotment of the Land (34:1—36:13)

Part Three

AT THE GATE TO THE LAND

(22:2—36:13)

THE ISRAELITES HAD NOW ARRIVED at the gate to the promised land. Geographically that gate is located in 22:1 as by "the plains of Moab beyond the Jordan at Jericho." For the Israelites God would keep the gate closed until E day (entrance day) arrived. The delay was for the accomplishment of God's sovereign business at this crucial junction in the history of the Israelites. In the midst of new problems, the people would experience God's hand of vindication and judgment (22:2—25:18). For preparation for life in the new land, a new census must be taken, a new leader succeeding Moses identified, and the law of God finalized (chaps. 26—30; actually Deuteronomy contains the bulk of legislation given to the people at this time). Good strategy called for completing the disposition of the Transjordan (land on the east side of the Jordan where the Israelites were now settled) before crossing into Canaan proper (chaps. 31, 32). Finally, specifications were given as to the geographical distribution of the lands of Canaan, with an identification of cities of refuge, and a recognition of the stability of inheritances within the respective tribes (chaps. 34—36).

I. PROBLEMS (22:2—25:18)

When God promised to give the land of Canaan to His people, He did not say that this land of rest and plenty would come to them without battle or trial. There would be battles, but He would give victory. There would also be other trials, including internal problems, but through Him the Israelites could triumph. Today, victory in Christian living comes not without battles and trials. As long as the enemy of the Christian's soul is given permission, he will continue to attack from without, and also from within. But Christian rest and victory are attainable through the power and grace of Christ. The applications of this section of Numbers to the Christian's entering into victorious Christian living are numerous.

A. *Opposition from Without* (22:2—24:25)

This story of King Balak and the soothsayer Balaam has basically two main facts: (1) curse on Israel was sought (22:2-40), and (2) blessing on Israel was given (22:41—24:25). All the action took place outside the knowledge of the Israelites, for neither an Israelite nor a leader of the Israelites was an actor in the narrative. A point seems to be made of this fact as the author of Numbers closed the narrative by the pungent last sentence describing the two main actors returning unobtrusively to their own habitations: "And Balaam rose up, and went and returned *to his place;* and Balak also went *his way*" (24:25).

The three main actors of this story are Balak, king of Moab; Balaam, a soothsayer of Mesopotamia; and God. That Balaam had some genuine power in the magical art of exorcism, like that of the Jewish exorcists of the

New Testament, was apparent, though the messages he transmitted in this narrative were not received through those media. Through some contact with the spirit world he was able to make pronouncements about people and things, and he had a wide reputation for just that, as Balak revealed in his words, "I know that he whom thou blessest is blessed, and he whom thou cursest is cursed" (22:6). But Balaam was not a prophet of God nor a man of God, though the words he spoke in this narrative were prophetic words of divine truth. Actually Balaam became involved not because God called him to the task at hand but because a heathen king engaged his services. Then God, as is His way occasionally with those not His own, used the soothsayer for His own purposes to make Balak's evil desires backfire.

1. *Curse on Israel is Sought* (22:2-40)

Fear in the heart of King Balak initiated the action of this story. This king of Moab had not engaged in battle with the Israelites, for they had passed by his nation along its eastern border as they journeyed north. To his utter distress Balak saw how the Israelites had vanquished the Amorites to the north, and feared, now the northern lands were in their hands, that this great multitude of warriors would look back to the south again, and lick up all of Moab and the land of the Midianites to the east of Moab, "as the ox licketh up the grass of the field" (22:4). In self-defense Balak chose to use not arms of warfare but the powers of the spirit world, and this was the counsel he gave to the elders of neighboring Midian. With rewards in their hands, a group of elders of Moab and Midian reached Balaam with this short but potent request: "Curse this people" (22:6).

The story now takes on the form of an interplay between three factors: (1) the words of Balak, (2) the words of Balaam, and (3) the words of God.

When the elders reached Balaam, they told him the *"words of Balak"* (22:7). Those words were, "Curse this people" (22:6). If Balaam had been a true prophet of God, he would have known immediately what to answer. He eyed the rewards offered by the elders, and probably wished that God would give consent to the cursing. So the first seeds of his evil wishes are seen in *his words*, "Lodge here this night, and I will bring you word again, as Jehovah shall speak unto me" (22:8). But *God's words* to Balaam were not of those wishes: "Thou shalt not go with them; thou shalt not curse the people; for they are blessed" (22:12).

In the morning Balaam reported to the elders, but held back part of Jehovah's message. He told them that Jehovah refused to give him permission to go to Balak, but he did not explicitly state that Jehovah had said, "Thou shalt not curse the people; for they are blessed."

The second delegation sent by Balak to Balaam was more impressive, by number, status, and reward. Balak's request was still, "Come, curse this people," but the bribery offer was far more attractive: high position of honor, plus granting any request of Balaam (22:17). Balaam refused in word, but he could not escape the lure of such great rewards. Because he still "loved the hire of wrongdoing" (II Pet. 2:15), he kept negotiations open by suggesting a second overnight tarrying when he would consult with God again. God knew Balaam's heart, and His pedagogy now planned an experience which would awaken Balaam from his sleep of sin. God gave him permission to go to Balak on one condition: "Only the word which I speak unto thee, that shalt thou do" (22:20).

In the morning Balaam was on his way, exulting no doubt because he felt that he now had at least some chance to cash in on the offer of Balak. The attitude of his heart was definitely evil, as borne out by II Peter 2:15. The Numbers account reads, "But God's anger was inflamed *over his going*" (22:22, Berkeley Version), where the Hebrew construction for the italicized phrase suggests that it was his heart attitude as he traveled that incited God's anger. The strange events recorded in the verses that follow would bear this out. At three different places the angel of Jehovah stood in the path of the ass on which Balaam was riding. Each time the ass saw the obstacle and moved accordingly; each time the ass was rebuked by Balaam because he did not see the angel of Jehovah. Furthermore, when the ass spoke as a man, through a miraculous act of God (22:28), Balaam, as though overwhelmed with the intensity of the evil thoughts building up in his heart as he approached Balak, kept up casual conversation without amazement over an ass speaking. Finally, the Lord opened Balaam's eyes and seeing the angel of the Lord he bowed his head and fell on his face, responding, "I have sinned" to the angel's "Thy way is perverse before me." Though he offered to return to his home again, he was instructed by the angel to continue with the men, but to speak only the word that the angel of Jehovah would speak to him.

When Balaam with the princes of Balak approached the city of Moab, on the Arnon River, Balak went out to meet them. Now Balak's words of biting impatience resound: "Did I not earnestly send unto thee to call thee? wherefore camest thou not unto me?" (22:37). Subdued by his last experience with God, *Balaam's words* were simply, "Have I now any power at all to speak any thing?" (22:38). And *God's words* are given preeminence, "The word that God putteth in my mouth, that shall I speak" (22:38).

2. *Blessing on Israel Is Given* (22:41–24:25)

From a purely quantitative standpoint, the words of God are given obvious preeminence in this story of Balak and Balaam, for chapters 23 and 24 for the most part are God's words of blessing on Israel as God revealed these to Balaam. The chapters contain four messages, sometimes called prophecies, delivered to Balak. Three were solicited by Balak; the fourth was given voluntarily by Balaam after he had been severely rebuked by Balak.

Balaam by profession was an augur, foretelling the future on the basis of omens or signs which he would see from phenomena of nature. This was a common heathen practice. And so it was that when the moment came for him to seek the first message from God, he sought out a "bare height" (23:3) where he might see omens. This he did for the second prophecy also (23:15). But for the third, "he went not, as at the other times, to meet with enchantments, but he set his face toward the wilderness" (24:1). Though Balaam sought omens from nature on the first two occasions, the message given to him was not from the omen, but from God Himself: "And the Lord put a word in Balaam's mouth. . . ." (23:5, 16).

Chapters 23 and 24 are two of the brightest chapters in the book of Numbers. Scores of wonderful things are said about Israel, mainly prophetical. The dark sins of the past were forgotten; only happy deliverance from Egypt was cited. Israel was about to enter the promised land. The heathen nation of Moab desired to curse it out of existence. Unknown to the Israelites, God gave verbal testimony to this enemy of Israel that His people should not be cursed but blessed manifoldly. How often God has defeated the enemy of a child of His even when that child has been unaware of the opposition!

First Discourse (22:41–23:12). Looking down upon the hosts of Israelites from a high vantage point, Balaam prepared to receive the first word from God. Balaam instructed Balak to offer a bullock and ram on each of seven altars, a procedure common to heathen ceremonies of adjuration. Then he went alone to a bare height, where God bypassed his heathen profession of augury and spoke directly to him, giving him the very words that he should deliver to Balak (23:4, 5). In essence, the message was that Balaam could not fulfill Balak's request to curse Israel, because (1) God had not cursed Israel; (2) Israel was a distinct and unique nation, separated from heathen ways, with a unique destiny (23:9); (3) Israel was mighty in number; (4) Israel was righteous (23:10). Such an answer, of course, angered Balak.

Second Discourse (23:13-26). Hoping that omens seen in a different locality would lead Balaam to bring a word of cursing on Israel, Balak led Balaam to the top of Pisgah, at a place called "field of watchers" or "spies" (*Zophim*). The procedure of offerings, Balaam going off by himself, and his meeting God was then duplicated, and Balaam returned with the second communication. As an answer to Balak's hope that God had changed His mind, the message was, "God is not a man, that he should lie, neither the son of man, that he should repent" (23:19). God was doing what He had said He would do. That is, to His people in the midst of whom He could

dwell because iniquity was atoned for and wiped out
(23:21), God could give (1) deliverance out of bondage,
as in Egypt (23:22); (2) direct revelation of His ways
and means ("At a proper time it shall be stated to Jacob,
yes, to Israel what God has brought about," 23:23,
Berkeley Version) rather than communication through
sorcery or witchcraft; (3) strength and power over all
enemies (23:24).

On hearing this second word from God, Balak wished
he had not solicited Balaam's help at all: "Neither curse
them at all, nor bless them at all" (23:25). But this
momentary exasperation gave way to a third and final try
to secure the desperately desired curse on Israel.

Third Discourse (23:27—24:13). Stubborn Balak per-
sisted and asked for another communication. Perhaps his
experience in the past made him think that soothsayings
of professional augurs were fickle and changeable; and
so he led Balaam to a third place, "peradventure it will
please God that thou mayest curse me them from thence"
(23:27). The place was a spot on top of Mount Peor,
overlooking the steppes of Moab, where Israel was encamped.

By this time the experiences of meeting God on the
two previous occasions, and hearing in detail God's blessings on Israel, had convinced Balaam that God would
have the last word. "When Balaam perceived that it
pleased the Lord to bless Israel" (24:1, Berkeley Version), he did not look for omens as on the previous occasions, but turned his face in the direction of Israel,
and saw their camp in order by tribes. At this moment
the Spirit of God came upon him, a new experience for
him. Earlier, the Lord had given him the words to say
without this ministry of the Spirit of God. Now, with

the Spirit of God "upon him" (24:2), his experience was more like that of God's prophets, who received their message by way of the Spirit without external media. The first part of his discourse corroborated this when he said that he saw "the vision of the Almighty" (24:4) with closed eye (24:3).

The discourse itself described by means of many striking figures a prosperous and victorious Israel under the hand of God, blessed for the ages to come. It ended with a reference to the original covenant given to Abraham: "Blessed be every one that blesseth thee, and cursed be every one that curseth thee" (24:9; cf. Gen. 12:3; 27:29).

This third discourse, with its almost twenty blessings declared on Israel, was the breaking point for Balak's persistence. His anger kindled, he rebuked Balaam and sent him back to his country. But Balaam, very likely still inspired by the Spirit of God to speak as he had done in his third discourse, had the last word; and so, unsolicited, he recited what Israel would do to Moab and other surrounding nations at a later time (24:14).

Fourth Discourse (24:14-25). Whereas the third discourse was predominantly positive in describing the blessed state of Israel, the last of Balaam's sayings was predominantly negative with reference to the heathen nations, in that it foretold their ultimate destruction at the hands of the Israelites. Moab would be smitten by a "star" that would come forth out of Jacob, one of the great Old Testament prophecies, heralding in its ultimate fulfillment the coming of Christ. Edom and Seir would also fall. Amalek, the first of nations, would eventually be destroyed. The Kenites, Asshur, and Eber would also see destruction. "Alas, who shall live when God doeth this?" (24:23).

Although, as noted earlier, Israel was apparently not aware of Balaam's messages at the time of their delivery, they were to become acquainted with them eventually, since Moses would be incorporating them in the Torah. Balaam's messages therefore were used eventually to instruct the Israelites as to their victorious future in the face of insurmountable opposition.

This was enough. The word of God had spoken, and there was none to deny it. Even the mouthpiece of God, Balaam, left the scene with the intention to return to his place, and Balak, who despised the word of God, "also went his way" (24:25).

In the earlier chapters of Numbers God vindicated His leaders in the midst of rebellion from within. Now God had vindicated His people and protected them from enemies from without. No man can thwart His sovereign purposes. The nation of Israel, about to enter the land of plenty, had much more to learn about their gracious and omnipotent protector, even in experiences of trouble unknown to them.

B. *Opposition from Within* (25:1-18)

The ways of Satan, the archenemy of the soul, are devious and subtle. When one strategy fails, he is quick to engage another. This is vividly illustrated in the story of Israel in these chapters. First came the plot to destroy Israel by way of a curse. It was a clear-cut case of opposition from without. The deliverer of Israel was not Balaam, though his lips uttered words of blessing, but God, whose zeal to bless remained undiminished.

When the story ended, Balaam departed to go to "his place." Though God used his lips as His mouthpiece, Balaam's heart was far from right. Forfeiture of high honor and prizes must have made him boil with fury. Now he conceived how he might cause Israel to fall by another device, the common heathen admixture of licentiousness and idolatry. Balaam's name does not appear in the record of chapter 25, because the sin of the people is the point of attention. But 31:16 identifies him as the one who gave the counsel that caused Israel to sin against God at this time. The strategy of opposition from without had failed; now the strategy was that of opposition originating from without but working from within: *let the Israelites themselves cause their own downfall,* through the lust of the flesh.

1. *The Sin*

The Moabites and Midianites, allied nations, were co-instigators of Israel's sin (25:1, 17, 18; 31:16), and therefore appear interchangeably in the account of Numbers. While the Israelites were encamped at Shittim, in the steppes of Moab, the daughters of Moab enticed the men of Israel to their services and activities in the idolatrous worship of Baal of Peor, which included eating, ritual, and prostitution. It was not a matter of isolated cases of defection, but wholesale traffic: "And Israel joined himself unto Baal-peor" (25:3). So flagrant and open was the sin, that before the very eyes of Moses and the congregation of Israel, as these still righteous ones were weeping over the judgment of God already fallen, an Israelite, Zimri, led a Midianitish woman, Cozbi, into a tent for immoral purposes (25:6, 7).

2. *The Judgment upon Israel*

His anger kindled against Israel, God commanded Moses to slay those who had been leaders in the sin, and to impale their bodies upon stakes against the sun, that is, in public exhibition under the open skies. Hanging there "before the Lord" (25:4, Berkeley Version), the slain bodies were to be signs to the people for atonement and appeasement of God, "that the fierce anger of Jehovah may turn away from Israel" (25:4). As another part of the judgment (identified in this chapter as a "plague," 25:8), Moses instructed the judges to slay every man guilty of the sin. Before the plague was stayed, twenty-four thousand died. (Paul's number of twenty-three thousand [I Cor. 10:8] may not include those first "crucified.") Included also in God's judgment was the slaying of Zimri and Cozbi. Associated with their judgment was the sad fact that the record of their shame includes the names of their fathers, who were princes among their people. Zimri is identified as "the son of Salu, a prince of a fathers' house among the Simeonites," and Cozbi as "the daughter of Zur; he was head of the people of a fathers' house in Midian" (25:14, 15).

3. *The Atonement*

It is very clear from the record that atonement, or the staying of the plague of punishment (25:8), came by representative death and representative righteousness. The representative death is seen in the hanging or impaling of the guilty leaders which would turn away God's wrath from Israel (25:4). The representative righteousness is seen in the actions of Phinehas, grandson of Aaron the priest, who out of jealousy for his God slew Zimri and Cozbi with a spear for their sin (25:7, 8). God told

Moses that it was because Phinehas "was jealous for his God" that atonement was made for the children of Israel (25:13). For Phinehas' divine zeal God gave a "covenant of peace," assuring him and his seed the ministry and privilege of an "everlasting priesthood" (25:12, 13).

4. *The Judgment Upon Midian*

Lest the seducers of the Israelites absolve themselves of guilt, God commanded Moses to "vex the Midianites, and smite them" (25:17) as judgment for their sin of defiling His people. Thereby the heathen nations could clearly see the universal truths about sin and its judgment. Before entering Canaan the Israelites would fulfill this command to smite the Midianites (chap. 31).

* * *

The toll of Balaam's evil counsel was costly to Israel. Twenty-four thousand empty places in the families spoke a loud and sober message to the people as they reflected on this most recent catastrophe. They must guard the citadels of the heart from the enemy that was without, and they must search the secret places of the heart for the enemy that was within. Never must they feel self-confident. Surely their flesh was weak. The law of God must be their guide, and trust in God their only hope.

II. PREPARATION (26:1—30:16)

The next five chapters record the last-minute preparations made on the eve of E day. A new census was taken in anticipation of assigning land to the families of the tribes, a new leader was identified in Joshua, and the law of God concerning offerings was brought into focus in a finalized form.

A. *New Census Taken*—Organization (26:1—27:11)

1. *The Census* (26:1-51, 63-65)

While the census of chapter 1 was taken primarily for organizational purposes for the anticipated wilderness journey and battles which were inevitable, this census had a different purpose. It was true that the mustering anticipated battles yet to come, and those numbered were such as were "able to go forth to war," over twenty years of age (26:2). But the primary purpose of the numbering was to ascertain how the land of Canaan would be allotted to the different tribes. Hence this census enumerated the *families* of the various tribes, which was not the case in the census of chapter 1.

Under the leadership of Moses and Eleazar, the census showed the following tallies for the tribes:

Reuben	43,730	Issachar	64,300
Simeon	22,200	Zebulun	60,500
Joseph-Manasseh	52,700	Benjamin	45,600
Joseph-Ephraim	32,500	Dan	64,400
Gad	40,500	Asher	53,400
Judah	76,500	Naphtali	45,400

The grand total was 601,730, slightly less than the Sinai count of 603,550. All those originally counted, except Joshua, Caleb and Moses, had died (26:63-65). Why the progeny of such a large original number was not larger over a period of forty years is explained partly by the mass plagues and slayings, and partly by the extreme hardships under which the people lived during the wilderness years.

2. *Principles of Land Assignments* (26:52-62)

After the enumeration of the population of each tribe,

directions were given for distributing the land among the tribes: (1) each tribe was to be given a territory proportionate to its population (26:54); (2) the location of the territory was to be determined by lot (26:55), the lot not determining the size but its relative location; (3) each land was to bear the name of the ancestor of the tribe (26:55).

The Levites, numbering 23,000, were not assigned any land inheritance (26:57-62), as was earlier stipulated by God (18:23).

3. *Rights of Heiresses* (27:1-11)

Zelophehad, the son of Hepher, of the families of Manasseh, had no sons, but five daughters: Mahlah, Noah, Hoglah, Milcah and Tirzah (26:33; 27:1). Since the father had died without leaving a male heir, an inheritance of land did not apply here, and the family name would normally cease to exist. The daughters, in justifiable family pride, appealed to Moses for an inheritance of land to be given them in the name of their father which they could perpetuate under his name for the generations to come. Since this was a procedure without precedent, Moses "brought their cause before Jehovah" (27:5), who answered that the daughters had a just claim to the inheritance of their father (27:7). Then, for the record and for like future situations, God amplified the laws of inheritance in the event the earlier-named heir was not living: his son, his daughter, his brethren, his father's brethren, "his kinsman that is next to him of his family" (27:8-11). In this law of inheritance two principles were made prominent: (1) the family name, worth, and heritage perpetuated itself, and was not easily dissolved; (2) the dignity of woman, with reference to her being an integral part of the family, was preserved.

B. *New Leader Identified*—Leadership (27:12-23)

The time for the fulfillment of the judgment of Moses' sin at the waters of Meribah (20:10-13) was now at hand. Because Moses had failed to sanctify God before the eyes of the children of Israel, he, with Aaron, was not allowed to enter Canaan with his people. He was instructed by God to ascend the mountain of Abarim, a mountain range forming the Moabitish tableland, to a point called Mount Nebo, that he might have a view of the promised land before his death. It was a breathtaking view (Deut. 34:1-3) and was perhaps the scene of the greatest emotional experience Moses had in his lifetime. (Deut. 32:48—34:12 gives a more complete description of this event and of Moses' subsequent death and burial; the contents of the entire book of Deuteronomy are chronologically located during these days of preparation for entering the land of Canaan.)

Typical of the selfless heart of Moses, his response was not one of self-pity or mourning (read his song of blessing in Deut. 33), nor even expression of what must have been excitement over having God show him all the lands of inheritance. His immediate concern was for his people, that they be "not as sheep which have no shepherd" (27:17). Though he must have long ago expected that Joshua, his military captain, would be his natural successor, he did not presume the prerogative of appointment but asked Jehovah, "the God of the spirits of all flesh," to appoint a man to lead the people in their private and public life (27:16, 17).

God's choice was Joshua, a man in whom the Spirit dwelt, to whom Moses was to impart of his honor and dignity, as he gave him a charge before Eleazar and the leaders of the people (27:18-20). There would never be another prophet in Israel like Moses, whom "Jehovah knew face to face" (Deut. 34:10), and so Joshua, though "full of the spirit of wisdom" (Deut. 34:9), was given direction to use a revelatory source in making the supreme decisions of the affairs of Israel. That source was the Urim and Thummim (lit. "lights and perfections"), which were probably glistening stones on the priest's breastplate representing his function of determining the counsel and will of God. Joshua, in other words, was to consult Eleazar in making high-level decisions.

And Moses, aged 120, a mature man of God and faithful leader of His people through agonizing years of tribulation, still in prime physical condition (Deut. 34:7), who would have loved to be there when his people finally crossed the Jordan into the land of rest, unflinchingly obeyed his Master to the very end, and "*did as Jehovah commanded him*" (27:22). Before his actual death, recorded in Deuteronomy, Moses was to manifest this obedient attitude in a few more tasks as God's servant.

C. *Law of God Finalized*—Spiritual Life (28:1— 30:16)

1. *Law of Offerings* (28:1—29:40)

The real key to successful conquest of Canaan and happy living within its borders was *continual fellowship with God.* Hence it was that God at this time presented to the new generation by way of Moses a finalized and complete set of regulations for offerings, most of which had already been given at Sinai. Their observance would encourage an intimate worship of God by the people in the land (cf. Exod. 23:14-17; 29:38-42; 31:12-17; Lev. 23; Num. 25:1-12).

The offerings described in these chapters were: (1) daily (28:1-8); (2) Sabbath (28:9, 10); (3) new moon—"beginnings of your months" (28:11-15); (4) Feast of Unleavened Bread—in connection with the Passover (28: 16-25); (5) Pentecost—Feast of Weeks (28:26-31); (6) new moon of the seventh month—the new year (29:1-6); (7) Day of Atonement (29:7-11); (8) Feast of Tabernacles (29:12-39).

The following observations will serve to point out some of the prominent aspects of the offerings:

a. The offerings were not man-instituted nor man-desired; they were God's: *"My oblation, my bread* for *my offerings* made by fire, of a sweet savor *unto me,* shall ye observe to offer *unto me* in their due season" (28:2). By bringing the offerings to God the people were symbolically yielding themselves to Him.

b. The substratum of all the offerings was the daily offering. Day by day, in the morning and evening, he-lambs were to be offered for a "continual burnt-offering" (28:3), to emphasize the basic truth that fellowship with God was not to be a spasmodic thing, but a continuous reality. Even on the days of Sabbath and festal offerings, the daily offerings were to be observed.

c. The fundamental type was the burnt offering, which symbolically represented the yielding of the person to God.

d. All the feasts of the year formed a cycle, emphasizing different truths of the fellowship. The last, the Feast of Tabernacles, emphasized joy and thanksgiving: it was the first feast following the great atonement. It was the feast of first-fruits, and also commemorated the former life of Israel in tents and booths. One remarkable feature in the procedure of this feast was a decrease in the number of bullocks offered, from thirteen down to seven, from the first day to the eighth. One plausible explanation is that as the intensity of the feast diminished, so the outburst of joy of a saint of God on the festive day took on the calmer expression, though no less real and deep, in the joys of everyday living with God after the festivities were over.

e. These prescribed feasts were to be supplemented by the vows and freewill offerings of individuals to be offered to God at any time (29:39).

* * *

The laws of offerings presented in these chapters formed a fitting bond between Sinai and Canaan. In between the two lands was a dark wilderness, where a disobedient generation perished. Now the laws of fellowship by offering recorded here set in motion again the communion which God once had with Israel and now hoped to enjoy again.

2. *Laws of Vows* (30:1-16)

Although the Israelites had already been given regulations concerning the objects and discharge of vows (Lev. 27), now God gave the leaders of the tribes, through Moses, instructions concerning when vows, especially those of women, were valid or were made void. The anticipation here was of a family situation in a land of plenty where a woman, with material abundance at her disposal, might in deep fervor over the laws of Sinai rashly and unfairly upset the household economy by vowing an overabundance of things in her worship.

The primary aspects of truth taught by the vows as described in this chapter were:

a. Vows to Jehovah were not made to be broken. "When a man voweth a vow unto Jehovah . . . *he shall not break his word*" (30:2).

b. Anyone might make a vow: man (30:2) or woman (30:3).

c. The vow could be a positive one, involving presentation of one's property to the Lord (the word *neder* is translated "vow"); or a negative one, involving some type of abstinence (the word *issar* is translated "bond") (30:2). Note that the Nazirite's vow of chapter 6 was called a *neder*, to emphasize the positive aspect of his vow, even though a negative aspect was involved.

d. Vows made by women of a household were subject to the judgment of the head of the household. This is understandable, since the head of the household was responsible for its physical sustenance, which rash and hasty vows of property, uncontrolled, could very quickly upset. Four examples are cited: (1) The vow of a young woman, unmarried and living in her father's house, could be vetoed by the father at the time the vow was made. If the vow was not disallowed at that time, the vow was in force (30:3-5). (2) The vow or "rash utterance" of a woman made while betrothed, and brought along with her into her ("upon her") marriage, could be disallowed by her husband at the time he learned of the vow; otherwise the vow was in force (30:6-8). (3) The vow of a widow or divorced woman was valid and uncontestable, for she formed a household in herself (30:9). (4) The vow of a wife could be made null and void by her husband at the time the vow was made; otherwise it was in force (30:10-12).

* * *

Vows were too sacred to be entered into lightly, hence God's strong and clear safeguards against the abuse of this sacred domain of worship. This truth God considered to be of such paramount importance for the family life in Canaan that He enunciated its specifics at this time.

III. TRANSJORDAN BUSINESS (31:1—32:42)

A. *Decimation of Midianites* (31:1-54)

Before crossing the Jordan into Canaan, the Israelites were to serve as God's agents in the judgment He had earlier declared against the Midianites (25:16-18). It was the last violent action Moses was to see before his death. The decimation of this nomad-like tribe of people had two purposes: (1) judgment for their sin in enticing the Israelites to their corrupt and immoral Baal-peor idolatry, inciting thereby the just wrath of Israel's God; (2) protection of the Israelites, especially those who would be living east of the Jordan, from any similar future seductions.

The record of Numbers states that *every* male (3:7, 17) and *every female except virgins* of the women and children (31:17) were killed, these virgins being taken captive. How then could there have existed a nation of Midianites later in the days of Joshua of substantial size to prevail against Israel seven years (Judg. 6:1-6)? The answer probably is that the Midianites slaughtered in Moses' time represented not the entire Midianite people, but Midianites in the vicinity of the Hebrew camp, living as a unit and in this respect correctly referred to in the

Biblical text in terms of totality. Their kinsmen, removed from the scene of battle on their pastoral wanderings—for they were of nomadic character—were apparently therefore the forebears of the Midianites of Joshua's day.[1]

The war against the Midianites was really God's war, executing His vengeance by means of the army of Israel (31:3). That it was such a "holy" war was visibly demonstrated in the fact that Phinehas, whose zeal for God's holiness had recently been spotlighted, was one of the attending leaders, carrying the alarm trumpets used in battle (alarm trumpets apparently being "the vessels of the sanctuary," the "and" of 31:6 having the intention of an explicative, i.e., our word "even"). The violent toll of human life (every adult male, 31:7; five Midian chiefs and Balaam, 31:8; every woman except virgins, 31:17; every male child, 31:17) can be justified only in the fact that this was *God's* holy judgment, not *man's* arbitrary retaliation.

The Midianite warriors were very likely unprepared for the twelve thousand Israelite men of war suddenly descending upon them. Even if prepared, their defeat was inevitable. The women and children, taken captive at first (31:9-12), were later slain at the command of Moses (with the exception of the virgins, "women—children," 31: 13-18) to protect the Israelites from any further defilement, and to prevent a future propagation of the Midianite race.

For their defilement by contact with dead bodies and defiled objects, the warriors were required to fulfill the requirements of the seven-day period of purification that Jehovah had given Moses earlier (31:21; cf. chap. 19).

[1]See Jamieson, Fausset and Brown, *A Commentary on the Old and New Testaments,* I, 603-605, for a discussion of the alleged exaggerations or discrepancies in this account.

As with all wars, there was the booty (*shalal,* "spoil" in goods) and the prey (*malkoach*) in man and beast. The remainder of the chapter describes their distribution (31:25-54). The prey of man and beast was equally divided among the two groups of warriors and congregation, recognizing equal deserving by both groups. The supply of this prey for the present physical needs of the Israelites—still travelers without a homeland—must certainly have been very timely, part of the divine timetable of gracious provision. From the allotment of prey to the warriors was a portion for the priests, and from the allotment to the congregation was a portion for the Levites.

ALLOTMENT OF PREY

	Warriors	*Priests*	*Congregation*	*Levites*
	(½)	(1/500)	(½)	(1/50)
sheep	337,500	675	337,500	6,750
oxen	36,000	72	36,000	720
asses	30,500	61	30,500	610
maidens	16,000	32	16,000	320

In gratefulness to God for victory in battle *without one casualty* (31:49), the leaders of the armies offered a sacrificial gift of all the articles of gold which the Israelites gathered from the Midianites, including ankle chains, bracelets, signet rings, earrings, and necklaces (31:50). (The warriors were allowed to keep other kinds of booty for themselves, 31:53.) The total value was 16,750 shekels. The gift, though described as given "to make atonement for our souls" (31:50), was not intended to cover any guilt, for there was no guilt. Rather, it was a gratitude gift, given "for a memorial for the children of Israel before Jehovah" (31:54).

So, purged of one potential threat to their spiritual
life, given physical sustenance for their present needs,
and reassured of the presence and help of their God
against any alien nations, the Israelites are about ready
to cross the Jordan into the promised land.

B. *Allotment of Transjordan Land* (32:1-42)

The Reubenites and Gadites, blessed with many herds
of cattle and beasts, were quick to look out for their own
interests. They saw the land of Gilead, the Transjordan
tableland reaching from the Dead Sea in the south to the
Sea of Galilee in the north, as perfect land for cattle.
To Moses, Eleazar and the princes, their proposal took
the form of two couplets: (1) Gilead is a land for cattle;
we have cattle (32:4). (2) Let us settle here; excuse us
from conquering Canaan (32:5).

The text does not reveal their heart motives, except as
these are implied in Moses' rebuke. Theirs was a danger-
ous suggestion, inviting schism and discouragement (32:
7, 9) in the ranks of Israel on the eve of E day. "Shall
your brethren go to the war, and shall ye sit here?"
(32:6). After citing the wilderness sin of the spies' dis-
couraging Israel from entering the land (32:8-13), Moses
thrust cutting indictment upon the Reubenites and Gadites when he said, "And, behold, ye are risen up in your
fathers' stead, an increase of sinful men, to augment yet
the fierce anger of Jehovah toward Israel" (32:14).

Rebuked by Moses, the cattlemen apparently took
counsel together, and returned to Moses with an alter-
nate plan, designed to satisfy both their desire for the
land and Moses' demand for equity among the tribes in
the rigors of conquest. In essence, the new proposal
called for (1) the land being given them; (2) their

going to war with the other tribes until all of Canaan had been conquered. Before leaving the land to cross the Jordan, however, the men would first have to build sheepfolds for their cattle and fortified cities for their wives and children (32:16, 17, 24-26). Moses, accepting their proposal, but not without warning against defection (32:23, 30), gave them permission to start building the cities and sheepfolds (32:24), and gave Eleazar, Joshua, and the leaders of all the tribes of Israel instructions to implement the plan.

It is at this point of the record that the half tribe of Manasseh is also cited as a recipient in the allotment of the Transjordan land(32:33), evidently because they had a decisive part in dispossessing the Amorites of the land (32:39-42). Bashan, the land of King Og, was included in the territory given these tribes (32:33). The names of the fortified cities with their sheepfolds, which the cattlemen built, are listed in 32:34-38.

Another internal crisis, quietly simmering in one faction of Israel because of the lust of the eye, was thus quickly extinguished by the gifted leader and man of God, Moses, who never did retire from duty as long as he was given breath.

IV. RECAPITULATION (33:1-49)

This part of the story of Numbers is inserted by Moses as a rehearsal of the past, for the sake of record. In the action of the Numbers account, the Israelites were now encamped "in the plains of Moab by the Jordan at Jericho," about ready to cross over for the conquest. Recapitulation was in order, therefore, and so Moses recorded the list of the journeys of the Israelites from the time of their exodus from Egypt (33:1) to their reaching the Jordan (33:49):

Verses 1-15: the marches from Egypt to Sinai

Verses 16-36: twenty-one encampments from Sinai to Kadesh (encampments of verses 19-36 are those of the thirty-seven years of wandering)

Verses 37-49: from Kadesh to the Jordan

One impression cannot escape the student who has followed the account of Numbers up to this point, that is, the long-suffering grace of God in preserving a people as He had originally promised, through all the experiences of this vast number of places.

Even so, the rest-life which the Christian may enjoy in this life depends ultimately on the same grace of God, who offers to give such happy living to His own children.

V. ANTICIPATION (33:50—36:13)

The eyes of the Israelites were now directed across the Jordan, but not without mixed feelings. For the land they saw was a land of enemies. But it was also God's land, a land of His promise. It was the purpose of God that they should see it as such, two lands, as they prepared to enter it.

A. *The Task at Hand* (33:50-56)

God always makes the vital issues clear. The deep mysteries and vague peripheral truths are revealed at later times, if at all; but the basic truths of life and death, such as salvation, He makes simple and clear.

Even so, there could be no question now in the minds of the Israelites what God wanted them to do. If they were to possess Canaan for a dwelling place as He had promised (33:53), they were to (1) drive out *all* the inhabitants of the land from before them; (2) destroy *all* their figured stones and molten images; (3) demolish *all* their high places (33:52). Any heathen inhabitants allowed to remain would be as pricks in their eyes and thorns in their sides, vexing them with the judgment of God (33:55, 56).

The lesson is clear as applied to the life of rest in the book of Hebrews. All other conditions for this happy life may have been fulfilled; nevertheless, old habits of sin and persistent idols of the heart will continue to vex the Christian and cause him to forfeit the manifold blessings which would otherwise be his.

B. *Allotment of the Land* (34:1—36:13)

1. *Outer Limits of the Land* (34:1-29)

The general designation of the lands given to Reuben, Gad and the half tribe of Manasseh was previously made. Now God showed Moses the boundaries of the remainder of Canaan yet to be distributed among the nine and one-half tribes. The *southern border* reached from the southern tip of the Salt Sea (Dead Sea) to the great (Mediterranean), by way of the ascent of Akrabbim, following the general valley depressions toward Kadesh-Barnea, thence out to the sea (34:3-5). The *western border* was simply the Great Sea (34:6). The *northern border* is very difficult to determine, but apparently included areas of the Hermon mountain range, parts of which were never to be possessed by the Israelites (34:7-9). The longest section of the *eastern border* was the Jordan valley, from the Sea of Chinnereth (Galilee) to the Salt Sea.

The upper boundaries are not identifiable with accuracy (34:10-12).

The precise way in which God defined the boundaries showed His meticulous exercise over the details of His gifts. Even as He knew each soul of His people, so He was acquainted with the fields and mountains and valleys which would be their dwelling places.

So important was the task of assigning the land inheritances to the different tribes, God Himself chose the committee which was to function here. (The actual assignment of lands is recorded in Josh. 13–19). In addition to Eleazar the priest and Joshua, one prince of every tribe was named (34:16-29). An interesting observation is the translation of each personal name:

Judah: Caleb, "attacker, seizer"
Simeon: Shemuel, "heard of God"
Benjamin: Elidad, "loved of God"
Dan: Bukki, "reverer of Jehovah"
Joseph-Manasseh: Hanniel, "grace of God"
Ephraim: Kemuel, "assembly of God"
Zebulun: Elizaphan, "whom God shields"
Issachar: Paltiel, "whom God rescues"
Asher: Ahihud, "friend of union"
Naphtali: Pedahel, "whom God redeems"

2. *Levite Cities* (35:1-8)

As God had earlier arranged, the Levites were not to receive a land inheritance as the other tribes would, for God was their possession. However, they had to have a place to live, as well as pasturage, as limited as these might be, for the live cattle and beasts given to them. Hence the provision of assigning forty-eight towns in

which they might dwell, the suburbs of which were to be
for pasture and grazing. Notice, a whole town was not
given the Levites, but as much as was needed for dwelling places (see Lev. 25:32-34). Measured from each wall
of the city, the outer limits of pasture land extended one
thousand cubits (a cubit was eighteen inches). This
would mean that each of the four outermost field lines
of the pasture lands—north, south, east and west—was
two thousand cubits long plus whatever was the length
of the city wall (35:4, 5; the length of the city wall would
vary, and so was not included in the dimension here).
The number of Levite cities allotted from each tribe
was proportional to the size of the tribe (35:8; see Josh.
21).

Thus God made provision for scattering the savor of
salt of the Levites' ministry throughout the land of Israel.
Serving in the things of the sanctuary, and walking daily
in the midst of the people, they helped to keep in bright
view before the Israelites the covenant and law and testimony of Jehovah, and the necessity of living by them.
Also, as a constant reminder of the intimate relationship
of God's written *law* and the workings of His *grace*, six
of the Levite cities were designated as places of refuge
for a manslayer fleeing from his avenger (35:6), fleeing,
as it were, into a city of God to plead His mercy.

3. *Cities of Refuge* (35:9-34)

The marriage of God's righteousness and grace is
vividly demonstrated in the reason and provision for
cities of refuge which the Israelites were to designate
in the new land.

God's Righteousness. The end of this chapter leaves
no doubt as to the principles involved (35:33, 34). When

a man was slain, intentionally or unintentionally, blood was shed. Shed blood polluted the land. Expiation for that blood could be made only "by the blood of him that shed it" (35:33). God would be dwelling in the midst of Israel; therefore, to remove the defilement from the land, provision for legal expiation would have to be made, or God could not dwell there.

God's Grace. The six appointed cities of refuge, three on each side of the Jordan (35:14), were God's answer to the expiation for an unintentional slaying. The pertinent observations to be made here are:

a. The right of revenge by the slain man's kin was recognized (see Gen. 9:5, 6). For premeditated murder, in the sight of at least two witnesses (Num. 35:30), there was no refuge for the slayer (35:16-21), not even the hope of "ransom" by money (35:31).

b. For accidental slaying, "without enmity," "without lying in wait" (35:22, 23), there was a legal guilt of shedding blood, but no moral guilt. The latter was the reason for blood vengeance not being due. (See Deut. 4:41-43; 19:1-13; Josh. 20:7 for identification of the cities of refuge.)

c. Trial by the leaders of the congregation determined whether the slaying was accidental or not (35:12, 24, 25; see Josh. 20:4 ff. for a detailed description of the procedures followed). If accidental, the slayer was committed to live in the city until the death of the high priest; he could not be freed by ransom (35:32); and he forfeited protection from the avenger by leaving the city before the prescribed time.

d. The legal guilt of the unintentional slaying was ultimately expiated in the death of the high priest, for the slayer was required to dwell in the city of refuge "until the death of the high priest, who was anointed with the holy oil" (35:25). As mediator and representative of the people, the high priest in his death was thus shown to be the legal cause for justification of the shedder of blood. The demand for expiation was fulfilled, and the slayer was now not only saved from the wrath of the avenger but fully liberated to return to his own home.

4. *Preservation of Land Inheritances Within Tribes* (36:1-13)

God's promise of the land of Canaan to the families or tribes of Israel was a promise of perpetual inheritance. For this to remain such a land, divided among the families, all dissolving agents had to be neutralized. The example described in this closing chapter of Numbers serves as a fitting conclusion to the book, emphasizing the importance of God's people not committing themselves to anything that would dissolve the basis for continued divine blessing.

The recently given law of inheritance to daughters of sonless fathers (26:33) appeared to the tribe of the sons of Joseph to endanger the stability of the inheritance; for if the daughters (in this instance, the daughters of Zelophehad) married into another tribe, the land would be transferred to that tribe, the transaction being permanently confirmed in the year of jubilee (36:1-4). Ultimately such a situation would very easily dissolve the individual identity of the tribes themselves.

Moses saw their concern as a justifiable one, and interpreted the law, "according to the word of Jehovah" (36:5, 6), as including the vital commandment that the heiresses were to marry men of their choosing only from *the tribe of their father* (36:6). Thus no inheritance could move from tribe to tribe; the borders of the lands were permanently fixed by law of God. As with the other events in the concluding chapters of Numbers, this last event was one of obedience to God's commands: "Even as Jehovah commanded Moses, so did the daughters of Zelophehad . . ." (36:10).

Thus direction was given for the preservation of the land constituency of the tribes of Israel, who were soon to settle down in the long-anticipated land of promise. The worst thing that can happen to a promise is the dissolution of its blessings in the course of their fulfillment. Hence the command of unmixed marriages.

As a concluding verse to the last section of Numbers, and therefore to the entire book, Moses bestowed a Sinaitic-like importance to the directions and commandments given the Israelites "in the plains of Moab by the Jordan at Jericho," for they were all "commandments and . . . ordinances which *Jehovah* commanded" (36:13).

CONCLUSION

THE HISTORY of the book of Numbers has taken the nation of Israel from Mount Sinai to the plains of Moab, opposite Jericho, on the verge of their entrance into the promised land. First it was a brief journey in the dark unknown, demanding the utmost in trust and patience. Then it was a long aimless wandering in the judgment of tribulation, consuming the original generation over a period of years. Finally it was a new and swift journey by a new generation with a few of the old leaders, reviving the hopes of the nation to appropriate the original promise of a land of rest and blessing.

As Numbers closes, the people could expect to hear the trumpet soon as the signal to cross over the Jordan into the land. They would have to drive out the enemy, but their success was assured, for their God had said, "I will give it [the land] you" (10:29).

As surely as the land awaited an obedient people, so rest-living is offered God's people today: "There remaineth therefore a sabbath rest for the people of God" (Heb. 4:9). And the exhortation of Hebrews 4:11 indicates that the condition for such blessed living is the same: obedience, involving belief.

"Let us therefore give diligence to enter into that rest, that no man fall after the same example of disobedience."

SHORT BIBLIOGRAPHY FOR NUMBERS

Atlas of the Bible Lands. Maplewood, N. J.: C. S. Hammond and Co., 1959. Inexpensive atlas, with historical charts and illustrations.

GAEBELEIN, A. C. *The Book of Numbers.* New York: Our Hope, 1913.

GREENSTONE, JULIUS HILLEL. *Numbers.* Philadelphia: Jewish Publication Society of America, 1939.

HENRY, MATTHEW. *A Commentary on the Whole Bible,* Vol. I. New York: Funk and Wagnalls Co., n.d.

JAMIESON, ROBERT, FAUSSET, A. R., and BROWN, DAVID. *A Commentary on the Old and New Testaments,* Vol. I. Grand Rapids: Wm. B. Eerdmans Publishing Co., 1948.

KEIL, C. F., and DELITZSCH, F. *Biblical Commentary on the Old Testament, Pentateuch,* Vol. III. Translated by James Martin. Grand Rapids: Wm. B. Eerdmans Publishing Co., 1949. An excellent commentary, comprehensive, interestingly written. For the advanced student.

KERR, D. W. *Numbers (The Biblical Expositor).* London: Pickering and Inglis, 1960.

LANGE, JOHN PETER. *Commentary on the Holy Scripture, Numbers.* Translated by Philip Schaff *et al.* Grand Rapids: Zondervan Publishing House, reprint. An excellent commentary, with much helpful background material.

MACKINTOSH, C. H. *Notes on the Book of Numbers*. New York: Loizeaux Brothers, n.d. Written in a devotional style, with emphasis on spiritual application.

MACLAREN, ALEXANDER. *Exposition of Holy Scriptures, Exodus, Leviticus and Numbers*. New York: Hodder and Stoughton, n.d. Treats only certain sections of Numbers.

MACRAE, A. A. "Numbers," *The New Bible Commentary*. Edited by F. Davidson, A. M. Stibbs and E. F. Kevan. Grand Rapids: Wm. B. Eerdmans Publishing Co., 1953.

MARTIN, W. S., and MARSHALL, A. (eds.). *Tabernacle Types and Teachings*. London: Pickering and Inglis, n.d.

SMICK, ELMER. "Numbers," *The Wycliffe Bible Commentary*. Edited by Charles F. Pfeiffer and Everett F. Harrison. Chicago: Moody Press, 1962.

UNGER, MERRILL F. *Introductory Guide to the Old Testament*. Grand Rapids: Zondervan Publishing House, 1951.

YOUNG, EDWARD J. *An Introduction to the Old Testament*. Grand Rapids: Wm. B. Eerdmans Publishing Co., 1949.

Moody Press, a ministry of the Moody Bible Institute, is designed for education, evangelization and edification. If we may assist you in knowing more about Christ and the Christian life, please write us without obligation to:
Moody Press, c/o MLM, Chicago, Illinois 60610.